Children at the Center

A Workshop Approach to Standardized Test Preparation, K–8

Kathe Taylor
and
Sherry Walton

HEINEMANN
Portsmouth, NH

HEINEMANN
A division of Reed Elsevier Inc.
361 Hanover Street
Portsmouth, NH 03801-3912
http://www.heinemann.com

Offices and agents throughout the world

The author and publisher thank those who generously gave permission to reprint borrowed material.

Library of Congress Cataloging-in-Publication Data
Taylor, Kathe.
    Children at the center : a workshop approach to standardized test preparation, K–8 / Kathe Taylor and Sherry Walton.
      p.   cm.
    Includes bibliographical references.
    ISBN 0-325-00095-6 (alk. paper)
    1. Test-taking skills—United States. 2. Demonstration centers in education—United States. 3. Educational tests and measurements—United States. 4. Norm-referenced tests—United States.
5. Education, Elementary—United States—Evaluation. I. Walton, Sherry. II. Title.
LB3060.57.T39   1998
371.26—dc21   98-36048
                                    CIP

Editor: Lois Bridges
Production: Melissa L. Inglis
Cover design: Catherine Hawkes
Manufacturing: Louise Richardson

Illustrations © 1998 by Pamelia Valentine
Photographs © 1998 by Domenico Spatola-Knoll

Printed in the United States of America on acid-free paper
02 01 00 99 98 ML 1 2 3 4 5

We dedicate this book to our families, who were extraordinarily patient with us as we wrote during our "spare" time, and especially to our daughters, Kathryn and Ashleigh (Sherry's), and Taylor (Kathe's). Thank you for letting us tell your stories.

Contents

Acknowledgments

This project began with teachers and students at two elementary schools in Olympia, Washington: Lincoln and Madison. Their willingness to explore issues of learning and assessment with us helped us keep children at the center as we designed the workshops. We thank them, and all the other teachers and children, who have used the workshop materials and generously offered feedback, advice, and ideas.

Introduction

Have you ever heard or been part of this conversation?

> **First Child:** Why do we have to take these tests?
>
> **Teacher:** It's just something we have to do.
>
> **Second Child:** I hate these tests, and I don't think I'll do well. They make me feel bad.
>
> **Teacher:** Don't worry, just do your best. The tests don't really matter.

But they do matter. Children's and teachers' lives are impacted by norm-referenced test scores. For reasons of accountability and economics, and despite trends toward performance-based methods of assessment, norm-referenced, multiple-choice tests are commonplace and likely to be in demand well into the next century.

This situation creates a practical and ethical dilemma for teachers who may feel that this type of assessment does not align well with their curriculum and with the ways their students learn and demonstrate their knowledge. Assessment, teaching, and learning should be inextricably linked. Yet norm-referenced, multiple-choice tests are a form of assessment that many teachers do not trust to accurately reflect their children's knowledge, do not consider relevant to their curriculum, or do not believe is congruent with their teaching practice. Teachers who base their curriculum on constructivist theory, in particular, find their teaching practice in conflict with a selected-response form of assessment. Nevertheless, many teachers have to administer norm-referenced tests, and the scores affect children's lives.

Both the test format and the ways test scores are used often lead to both immediate and long-term problems for many groups of children, including some girls, students of color, students who live in poverty, and students with particular learning styles. Yet, many teachers acknowledge that they don't have the background skills or knowledge to confidently interpret norm-referenced test scores. As a consequence, their ability to be effective advocates for children is compromised.

In this book we provide practical solutions that will help meet the needs of children and teachers faced with taking or administering norm-referenced tests. First, we demystify norm-referenced tests by clarifying the concepts and language test companies use to describe their development and interpretation. Our common-sense approach, field-tested with practicing teachers, enhances teachers' ability to make sense of test scores for their own benefit and for the benefit of parents and children.

Second, we describe in detail student-centered workshops teachers can use to make it possible for children to better reveal their knowledge on standardized multiple-choice tests. We built the field-tested workshops around a carefully sequenced set of experiences that help teachers and students explore different types of test questions. These explorations encourage students to construct an understanding of what the test questions really ask them to do. Through the examination and discussion of "correct" and "incorrect" responses, students develop a clearer sense of cues, sources of information, and ways to determine the "best" response.

For additional help beyond the scope of this book, teachers might consider contacting the National Center for Fair & Open Testing (FairTest),[1] which provides information, technical assistance and advocacy on a broad range of testing concerns. It is the only national organization working exclusively to end the overuse and misuse of standardized tests.

Why We Wrote This Book

We are passionate in our belief that teachers have a responsibility to help children become competent in the literacy format of a norm-referenced test. Still, we occasionally find ourselves wondering how two unabashedly constructivist educators ended up on this path.

To be honest, we once walked the high road. Each of us has encouraged preservice and inservice teachers to critically assess the uses and abuses of norm-referenced test scores. We have also advocated for their elimination. However, we reevaluated our stance when two unrelated events occurred. First, one of our African American graduate students made a pointed comment about tests and children of color. She said, "It doesn't matter whether the tests measure knowledge or not. When children of color can't do well on those tests, they can't get into good

[1]To contact FairTest, write: FairTest, 342 Broadway, Cambridge, MA 02139. FairTest's website: http://www.fairtest.org

PART ONE

Building the Bridge Between Assessment and Instruction

CHAPTER ONE

Co-opting Standardized Tests in the Service of Learning[1]

On any given day, an outsider could walk into this public elementary school and observe students actively engaged in learning. Students might be working in cooperative groups, studying independently, participating in discussions, presenting a portfolio of their work, or listening to a short teacher- or peer-led lesson. A reading or writing workshop might be in process. Students of different ages would be working together in the same classroom. Parents would be assisting students, and teachers would be guiding learning in myriad ways.

A scenario typical of many classrooms? Perhaps. As more teachers model instructional practice that reflects recent research on learning and as more states move to performance-based assessments, the nature of teaching, learning, and assessment is gradually changing. Still, this scenario would rarely be typical of an entire school. The coherent curricular, teaching, and learning philosophy common to this school originated ten years ago as a separate program within the school. The developmentally based program, designed to give students more responsibility for their learning, has expanded over the decade to include the entire school.

Despite the rich learning environment, and despite teachers' assertions that students routinely demonstrate their knowledge and skills, this school's median achievement test scores declined steadily for three years. Concerns about the declining scores led the teachers and principal to enlist our services for a classroom-based research study. Together we investigated a method of preparing students for standardized tests that would maintain the integrity of the school's curriculum and its methods of learning. This approach—a series of interactive workshops

[1]A large portion of this chapter, reprinted with permission, is from an article we wrote that was published in the September 1997 issue of *Kappan*.

for children—was successful in three ways. Teachers learned, children gained confidence and skills, and test scores improved significantly. Yet, there were mixed responses to the improved test scores. Elation was tempered by suspicion that the results were too good; whispers of cheating escalated to allegations of test-rigging, a charge lodged by a group opposed to the teaching practices of the school. In the midst of feeling good about the children's improved self-confidence and performance, we found ourselves wondering, "Why bother?"

As we searched for answers to this question, we remembered a response to a question a student asked Annette Kolodny. Kolodny, now a dean and faculty member at the University of Arizona, talked about the responsibility an education imposes, and replied rhetorically, "If you are not responsible for your knowledge, what on earth have we been educating you for?" Our renewed commitment to bother emerged from our belief that teachers need to use their knowledge of assessment in the service of children's learning. Although assessment entails much more than administering norm-referenced tests, knowledge of this form of assessment is critical and begins with understanding the uses and misuses of norm-referenced test scores. It broadens to an understanding of the ethical considerations inherent in designing test preparation interventions that protect the integrity of the tests *and* honor the integrity of curriculum, pedagogy, and children. Armed with this knowledge and the awareness that these tests are prevalent in children's lives, it is difficult to imagine anything less than a commitment to act. This chapter explores a successful intervention that connected a thinking curriculum and a traditional form of assessment and led one group of teachers to act.

Becoming Responsible for Our Knowledge

Norm-referenced, standardized tests, trusted by many as reliable and valid measures of student achievement, have been a routine part of American students' school experiences since the mid-1900s (see Figure 1.1).

The persistent call for educational accountability and the public's faith in quantitative comparisons have only increased the clamor for "objective" ways to measure student performance (Paris et al. 1991; Stewart and Bennett 1991). In addition, testing has become an enormously lucrative industry in the United States (National Commission on Testing and Public Policy 1990). For these reasons, and despite trends toward performance-based methods of assessment, norm-referenced, multiple-choice tests are commonplace and they probably will continue to be widely used for years to come. When superintendents' salaries are contingent on the achievement test performance of students in their district—an extreme example of accountability, but nevertheless a real one—the power of these tests is apparent.

Date	Event
1900	College Entrance Examination Board established. Administered essay exams to students entering northeastern schools; purpose to drive boarding school curriculum, not to select applicants.
1917	First mass administration of objective mental tests. *Army Alpha* used to select officer candidates from the pool of Army recruits. More than 1.7 million soldiers tested.
1923	*Stanford Achievement Test Battery* introduced.
1926	First experimental administration of the College Board's *Scholastic Aptitude Test* (SAT) to 8,000 high school students.
1931	*Metropolitan Achievement Test* introduced.
1933	Reynold Johnson parlays a childhood prank (scratching pencil marks on the outside of spark plugs to keep the engine from turning over) into a machine that could electrically sense whether pencil marks on a scoring sheet were in the right places.
1937	*Iowa Test of Basic Skills* (then known as the *Iowa Every Pupil Tests of Basic Skills*). First statewide test, and first battery to emphasize skills rather than subject matter.
1941	Scoring scale for College Board's SAT set based on performance of a norm group of test-takers.
1948	Educational Testing Service (ETS) created.
1957	*California Achievement Test* introduced.
1969	First administration of *National Assessment of Educational Progress* (NAEP).
1969	*Comprehensive Test of Basic Skills* introduced.
1963–1977	Average scores on *Scholastic Aptitude Test* (SAT) declined by a total of 81 points.
1983	The report, *A Nation at Risk*, produced by the National Commission on Excellence in Education, warned of a "rising tide of mediocrity" in public schools, and called for standardized achievement tests to be administered at major transition points from one level of schooling to another.
1994	SAT scoring scale recentered.
1995	46 states have assessment programs; 41 report using multiple-choice items as *part* of their state assessments.
1998	President Clinton and other leaders continue to call for rigorous national tests of each fourth-grade student's reading skills and eighth-grade student's mathematics skills.

FIGURE 1.1 Selected Events in the History of Norm-Referenced Tests

Those convinced that logic and persuasion will ultimately lead to the demise of state-mandated achievement tests might ask themselves how frequently substantial changes are made to long-standing public policies. The standardized testing industry and the general American public are unlikely to be moved by school reform advocates' criticisms of multiple-choice items on statewide tests. Forty-one states report using multiple-choice items as part of their state assessment programs (Bond, Roeber, and Braskamp 1996). Over time, alternative assessments may gain wider acceptance and a more prominent place in public education (Rothman 1995). However, as we work toward that time, we can better fulfill part of our responsibility to children by teaching them how to become more adept at showing what they know under standardized, multiple-choice conditions.

Tests matter in children's lives. Teachers who intend only to reassure their students when they say, "Don't worry, the tests don't really matter," actually mislead them. First, the tests *will* affect students' lives. Second, well-meaning reassurance may negatively affect students' motivation and does little to help children understand how to cope with feelings of fear and incompetence. Fear and lack of motivation both affect performance.

Educators often use test scores to make decisions about students. Achievement test scores may determine placement in subject-area tracks and in remedial and enrichment classes. They may also influence decisions about whether children should be advanced to the next grade level or retained. In some states, test scores "count" only if students take the test in English. Even though students may be able to demonstrate their knowledge when tested in their native language, they may be excluded from educational opportunities because they cannot demonstrate what they know when tested in English.

These issues of inclusion and exclusion are immediate consequences children experience. *Who* is included and excluded may have more to do with culture, style, gender, and test-taking skill than with what the student actually knows. *What* is included in the curriculum may have more to do with what is included on the tests than with a clear curricular philosophy about what is good for children. When test scores are used to define learning and knowledge, questions of equity may arise. For example, one study found teachers who served disadvantaged students to be under "greater pressure to improve test scores and . . . more driven to focus on test content and to emphasize test preparation in their instructional programs"—at the expense, perhaps, of other more relevant knowledge and skills (Herman, Abedi, and Golan 1994, 481).

Other long-term, negative consequences loom when we do not help children learn how to effectively negotiate a standardized test. Recent research suggests that repeated experiences with standardized testing, particularly for low achievers, have a "cumulative, negative impact on students that can be summarized in three general trends: growing disillusionment about tests, decreasing motivation to give genuine effort, and increasing use of inappropriate strategies" (Paris et al. 1991, 14).

The long-range consequences of lower "achievement" are serious. When a test score becomes the most important factor determining who gets included in and excluded from educational opportunities, *scores that accurately reflect students' knowledge and skill become imperative.* This fact alone should be reason enough to ask ourselves how we can responsibly and ethically prepare children for tests without compromising either the tests or important educational goals.

Ethical Considerations

One challenge in designing any sort of test preparation is to address the question of what kind of intervention is ethical—and from whose point of view. In the past decade, the meaning and ethics of test preparation have come under scrutiny. William Mehrens and John Kaminski ranked test preparation practices on a continuum of acceptability, while James Popham offered a set of ethical principles to judge the appropriateness of various practices (Mehrens and Kaminski 1989; Popham 1995). Researchers have reported the wide array of educators' opinions about the legitimacy of various practices, noting that different definitions of "cheating" may be affected by the reality that achievement test scores are often used for purposes for which they were not intended (Smith 1991; Urdan and Paris 1994; Nolen, Haladyna, and Haas 1992). States hold teachers accountable and judge schools on the basis of test scores that are not well understood and that may not accurately reflect what students in a particular school or district know and are able to do. Scott Paris and his colleagues captured the feelings of many teachers when they noted, "The paradox of public demand for a high-priced product that is poorly understood and used is frustrating to educators who feel powerless to alter the status quo" (Paris 1991, 14).

From a purely psychometric perspective, any intervention that causes the procedures and conditions to differ from those under which the norm group took the test poses a threat to external validity and undermines comparisons to the norm group (i.e., "pollutes" the inference). Even nonpsychometricians worry about which interventions are fair. Indeed, medical doctor John Cannell raised a stir when he called attention to the statistical impossibility that nearly all states were reporting scores on standardized achievement tests that were above the national average (Cannell 1988). He suggested that one explanation for this phenomenon was flagrant cheating through inappropriate test preparation.

Stances like Cannell's would be easier to support without reservation *if* standardized test scores were used only in the manner intended and *if* comparable conditions existed in all American schools. In fact, they are not and do not. For example, a story on National Public Radio quoted officials in one district as saying that they would receive more money from the state if they were able to "drag their test scores up from their below-average level." In addition, the principal stated frankly that "the best development scheme for small towns like this is some upwardly mobile school test scores." This district offers material incentives to students such as bikes, televisions, and gift certificates to encourage students to take the tests seriously (National Public Radio 1998).

When test scores are used inappropriately—to compare the adequacy of different schools or curricular approaches, to award merit pay to superintendents and teachers, to make decisions about whether to retain a student in a grade, or to allocate funds—the ethical framework broadens. The preeminent ethical question shifts from "How do we protect the integrity of the test?" to "How do we protect the integrity of the children?"

A Classroom-Based Study

Little in the literature directly addresses how to successfully intervene in ways that protect the integrity of the curriculum and the child while at the same time preparing children to become more effective at negotiating norm-referenced achievement tests. One ethnographic study focused on the incongruity of interjecting assessment practice into an "authentic" curriculum (McAuliffe 1993). Our classroom-based research study, on the other hand, focused on creating congruence between a view of learning that expects students to actively construct their own knowledge based on what they already know and through interactions with their environment and a form of assessment that permits students to recognize or guess predetermined right answers. The primary purpose for building this bridge was to aid children schooled in constructivist methods of learning to become more adept at showing what they know on norm-referenced, multiple-choice tests. A secondary purpose was to defuse the natural tension that arises when assessment and instruction are not aligned.

The credence given to a constructivist view of knowledge is based on research in a variety of fields that has helped clarify how learning occurs. This approach rejects the notion that knowledge can be broken down into isolated components that can be taught outside of the settings where that knowledge would normally be applied (Resnick and Resnick 1989). Teachers who embrace a constructivist philosophy teach foundation knowledge in the context of problems that require higher-order thinking. They are likely to use collaborative and interactive methods that encourage students to question, consider multiple perspectives, and pool their combined resources to arrive at well-thought-out conclusions.

Even though the trend is toward performance-based assessments, multiple-choice, norm- or criterion-referenced tests will probably coexist with performance-based assessments for a long time. Yet a constructivist approach calls into question the adequacy of multiple-choice tests for assessing student learning. The tests, with their format of single right answers, are based on theories that assume learning to be a collection of discrete skills and bits of knowledge. Yet teachers who neither think of learning in that way, nor use methods aimed at developing the skills the tests require students to demonstrate, still need to help their students prepare for these tests. This need is intensified because constructivist approaches present few opportunities for students to experience conditions common to standardized, multiple-choice tests, such as working without collaboration under timed conditions and seeking one right answer from a list of prepared responses.

To keep in line with the school's constructivist philosophy, we designed our study to build on the ways students commonly experienced learning in this school: working collaboratively to solve problems and taking into account multiple points of view. We used learning processes familiar to the students to help them construct an understanding of how to solve problems in the context of a norm-referenced achievement test. The preeminent process question that guided the study was: How do we design an intervention that protects the integrity of children, the curriculum, and the test? More specifically, could fourth- and fifth-grade students accustomed to constructivist teaching approaches learn ways to better demonstrate their knowledge within the less familiar context of a norm-referenced, multiple-choice achievement test? Could constructivist teaching approaches be used to help fourth- and fifth-grade students accomplish this goal?

The study began with five premises. First, a norm-referenced, multiple-choice test is a particular type of literacy format that students can learn to negotiate, just as they can learn to work in other types of literacy formats such as mystery stories, poems, recipes, etc. Second, children learn about new literacy formats by constructing their understandings through active learning; drill-and-practice interventions are inadequate and inappropriate. Third, carefully designed learning experiences based on the existing curricular principles of the school will support the integrity of the curriculum and of the children. Fourth, affective responses to test conditions influence performance. Fifth, students already have, or can learn, coping skills and problem-solving strategies to help them negotiate norm-referenced, multiple-choice tests and other unfamiliar situations.

These premises shaped the design of a series of interactive workshops to help students negotiate norm-referenced, multiple-choice tests. Seventy-nine students participated in the workshops, which teachers offered for approximately an hour each day over a period of two weeks. We assessed the effectiveness of this intervention in three ways: student self-reports, student performance on a norm-referenced, multiple-choice achievement test, and teacher self-reports. All of these assessments revealed substantial growth in students' abilities to monitor and adapt their emotional reactions to the test, in their abilities to use problem-solving strategies to select answers to test questions, and in teachers' understandings of how children reason through test questions of this type. In addition, teachers reported anecdotally that students felt calmer and more confident, asked fewer clarification questions, and fought less on the playground than they had during previous test weeks.

Further, student test scores significantly improved. The total battery, median normal curve equivalent (NCE) for the students who participated in the workshops was 65.7; in the previous year, students had posted a median NCE of 41. This was the most dramatic change among the twelve elementary schools in the district, with the next closest school moving from a median NCE of 46.2 in 1994 to one of 57 in 1995.

Some might argue that this result could be an anomaly, reflecting the accomplishments of an unusually bright group of students. However, when we looked at the scores of fifth-graders who took part in the workshops, we found two important results. First, we used a repeated measures analysis of variance to compare the scores of fifth-grade workshop participants with the scores they earned in fourth grade and found that their fifth-grade scores were significantly higher. Second, we compared these gains to those made by students randomly selected from schools throughout the district. When we looked at the fourth- to fifth-grade scores of this control group of students and compared them to those involved in the workshops, we found that the total battery scores of the students who had participated in the workshops increased significantly more than the scores of the students in the control group.

In both the fourth and fifth grades, the scores of students involved in the workshops improved significantly *only* in the curricular areas already emphasized by the school. In subjects such as language mechanics and spelling—areas the school does not emphasize—scores improved, but not significantly. This finding reinforced our belief that the intervention did not "teach to the test"; rather, children gained skills to more accurately reveal knowledge they already had.

The Costs of Action

The benefits of our intervention may appear obvious, but they were not without cost. We would like to leave you with the psychometric equivalent of ". . . and they lived happily ever after." However, given the political implications of statewide testing, the power much of the public is willing to attribute to test results, and the resistance some groups feel toward standardized testing, it is unlikely that the needs of all stakeholders can be met. Norm-referenced tests have acquired mythic proportions in defining the worth of children, teachers, and schools. Any intervention that challenges these expectations is unlikely to be universally approved.

The most serious cost of intervening in this school was that the reactions of key stakeholders in the community threatened to overshadow the educational needs of children. While many people were delighted with the results of the workshops, others expressed emotions ranging from concern to outrage. One group did not accept standardized tests as an important aspect of children's education and questioned whether the workshops were a good use of teaching time. Conflicting views about the appropriateness of standardized tests created tension in the school. The teachers who conducted the workshops were caught in the middle. They saw the benefits of the workshops for the children, but they also understood the parents' concerns, many of which they shared.

At the other end of the continuum of attitudes toward norm-referenced tests was a group of community members who valued these tests as a way to validate the success of a curriculum. These community members were also opposed to the curricular philosophy of the school and had pointed to the declining achievement test scores as evidence that the curriculum was not working. This group greeted the report of the improved test scores with charges of cheating, which increased the tension in the school.

We have subsequently offered these workshops at other schools without provoking such strong community reactions. Nevertheless, the situation at the first study site exemplifies the highly charged atmosphere that often surrounds standardized testing and has little to do with what or how children are learning. It underscores the inappropriate uses of test results, which occur at the expense of children. During the workshops and following the tests, the children and teachers clearly articulated the ways in which the children had learned to be better problem solvers. Yet the community conversation following the report of the test scores almost never addressed these results. It also ignored the fact that the workshops maintained the integrity of the curriculum, teacher professionalism, the children, and the test.

When ethical educators are accused of cheating, and when the needs of children get lost in political conversations, powerful forces are at work. So we return to our original questions: How can we as educators use our knowledge of assessment responsibly in the service of children and learning? Given the prickly nature of issues associated with norm-referenced tests, what can be gained by intervention, particularly with children of elementary school age? Why should we bother to act?

Why We Should Bother

We bother for many reasons, but perhaps this story expresses them most succinctly.

One of us has a daughter who appeared destined to become one of the few children in the country who couldn't ride a bike without training wheels. Seven-year-old Taylor had assessed the situation, determined that she could get hurt learning the skill, and announced firmly that she had no interest in acquiring it. No amount of support or encouragement budged her from her decision. Then one day she climbed on her bike and rode. When asked what made that day different and why on that day she thought she could ride, Taylor said, "Before, I didn't know I had it in me."

All children deserve to experience this discovery, to find out they have it in them to learn. The challenge for educators is to find ethical and equitable ways to promote these discoveries within *all* of the learning contexts children experience in the schools, including norm-referenced tests. Performing successfully on a norm-referenced test is certainly not the ultimate measure of learning. Yet we also know that performing *unsuccessfully* on norm-referenced tests can have long-term negative consequences on students' test-taking attitudes, motivation, and strategies.

When we help children to develop problem-solving techniques within the context of this type of assessment, we begin to meet the challenge of promoting learning in many school contexts. We co-opt the tests in the service of learning by decreasing the likelihood that norm-referenced tests will act as barriers to children's academic opportunities and by increasing children's facility with a testing format they will encounter repeatedly. This is important because scores from these tests often determine who will be included in and excluded from educational and economic opportunities. Put simply, we bother because for children the stakes are very high.

CHAPTER TWO

Who's "Norm" and What's He Doing in My Class?

A Primer on Norm-Referenced Tests

Stop! We know what you want to do. You want to skip this chapter. You flash back to the testing and measurement class in your teacher preparation program and it isn't pretty. Visions of norms, confidence intervals, and normal curve equivalents dance in your head. Sweat begins to break out on your forehead.

Okay, maybe we're exaggerating just a little, but it's been our experience that most teachers, initially at least, are less than enthusiastic about exploring norm-referenced tests. We think we have a way, though, to make this exploration interesting, engaging, and informative. This

FIGURE 2.1 Meet "Norm"

chapter focuses on what teachers need to know in order to understand norm-referenced tests *well enough* to advocate for their students and communicate responsibly to parents. It emphasizes broad concepts about test construction and interpretation, rather than statistical procedures; readers interested in knowing more about the mathematics of norm-referenced tests may want to consult other sources. This chapter will help you review your understanding of how norm-referenced test scores are interpreted, how the tests are constructed, and what conclusions can be reached about students' knowledge. By the end of this chapter you should know why "Norm" is in your class and how to make sense of him.

Who Is "Norm"?

"Norm" is our tongue-in-cheek name for the norm-referenced tests that are abundant in our public schools. Norm likes to think he's a '90s kind of guy although he's been around since the 1930s. Norm is in your classroom because Americans place great faith in numbers and believe that numbers can describe complex phenomena such as learning. This belief is so strong that we routinely make crucial educational decisions about children based on a particular set of numbers— norm-referenced test scores. Further, parents expect teachers to be able to explain the meaning and implications of these scores. However, in talking with teachers, we have found that they often express concern about their ability to translate test results into language parents find meaningful. In Chapter Three, we provide common scenarios and suggested responses to questions parents frequently raise, such as:

- What's a percentile?
- What does this 52 on my child's test report mean?
- How can my child score so high on this test and receive a "needs improvement" on her report card?
- Why are the average test scores at this school lower than the average scores at the school across town?

Self-Assessment as a Guide to Teaching and Learning

We have structured this chapter to reflect our belief that new learning builds on prior knowledge and experience. We present test information in three sections: "Making Sense of Norms," "Making Sense of Averages," and "Making Sense of Test Scores." At the beginning of each section, you will find several multiple-choice questions to help you assess your current knowledge about test construction and interpretation. We intend for you to answer these questions first and use them as a foundation for understanding the information in each section.

This strategy may be similar to approaches you use to introduce a new theme or topic of study. You may ask students to take a pretest or write or talk about what they already know and want to learn. You help students become engaged in the topic and assess their existing knowledge through such procedures. In your classroom, student self-assessment helps you adjust your curriculum to meet the students where they are developmentally, in their current knowledge, and in their current understanding or misunderstanding of the topic.

We cannot adjust the "curriculum" of this book. However, your responses to the multiple-choice questions that precede each section can serve as a self-assessment. You may gain a clearer sense about what you already know and what you need to learn. Each of the test questions has one best answer. In each section that follows, we provide information and background that might help you to better understand test construction, language, and interpretation.

Section One: Making Sense of Norms

Assessing Your Current Knowledge

Ready to have some fun? Please respond to each item. As you say to your students, "Do your best work . . ."

1. The *items* on a norm-referenced test are selected to
   A. represent the knowledge and skills students in your school should have mastered.
   B. help teachers make instructional decisions.
   C. reveal which children are at grade level.
   D. rank and sort children by their ability to answer test questions representing various fields of knowledge.
   E. make us crazy.

2. A national norm group
   A. is formed every year by a test company to assure that norms stay current for each test it publishes.
   B. provides the scores against which subsequent test-takers' scores are compared.
   C. consists of children from every state in the country.
   D. is all of the above.

3. Almost all norm-referenced tests are divided into subtests, such as language mechanics, math computation, and reading comprehension. Students receive a raw score on each subtest. A student's raw score
   A. on one subtest can be directly compared to his raw score on another subtest.
   B. is the number of items he answered correctly.
   C. is a half-baked estimate of performance; hence, the name "raw."
   D. is equivalent to the standard score divided by one hundred.

4. A student's test report stated that she had scored higher than 99 percent of fourth-grade students in the country. What does this statement mean?

   A. Her score was higher than 99 percent of other fourth-graders' scores in the country.

   B. Her score was higher than 99 percent of other fourth-graders' scores in her classroom.

   C. Her score was higher than 99 percent of other fourth-graders' scores in the norm group.

   D. Her score means that she has mastered 99 percent of the fourth-grade curriculum as represented by the norm group.

5. One of your students received a raw score that was equivalent to the seventy-fifth percentile based on local (district) norms, and to the fiftieth percentile based on state norms. This means:

   A. Students in your district must have performed better than students in the state norm group.

   B. Students in your district must have performed less well than students in the state norm group.

   C. The student's score can be interpreted as the average of the two percentiles; in this case, the average would be 62.5.

   D. The student performed better than 75 percent of students in the state.

   E. Who knows; who cares; who wrote this question?

Expanding Your Understanding of Norms

Two basic concepts will help you think about test construction. Both are directly related to an understanding of *norms*. The first specifies how and why test-makers select particular test items. The second describes how your students' scores are created.

Selecting test items

> The universe of knowledge is vast, but only a few test items will fit on a page.

Imagine a circle that represents all the knowledge that exists about a particular subject area, for instance, science. Now imagine that you are charged with creating a test that will tell you if children have that knowledge. You can't possibly ask them everything; nor can you reasonably expect children to know everything. What are you going to do?

If you worked for a company that creates tests, you would consult state curriculum guidelines, common textbooks, and experts in this subject area. Armed with this research, you and your colleagues would construct a large number of items that represent the knowledge identified by your resources that children at different ages are expected to acquire.

But here's the rub. These companies deliberately construct norm-referenced tests to sort and rank children's performances. Not only do the test items need to be representative of the subject area, they also need to create rankings of children that suggest some children know more than others. In order to select test items that accomplish both purposes, the test company administers the items to a sample of children and carefully analyzes their responses. They select some items for the published test that few children in the sample could answer. They choose others because many of the children answered them correctly. However, they rarely select items that all children answered correctly. Although these items may represent knowledge of the subject area, they are not useful in ranking children's performances.

This approach to choosing test items may be fundamentally different from the ways classroom teachers construct tests. Teachers are usually more interested in items that represent what the children have been learning and less interested in items that rank their students. With teacher-constructed tests, the potential exists for *all* children to correctly answer most of the items. That potential *does not* exist on a norm-referenced test. The diagram below shows how the knowledge standardized tests require from children can differ from that your curriculum provides them.

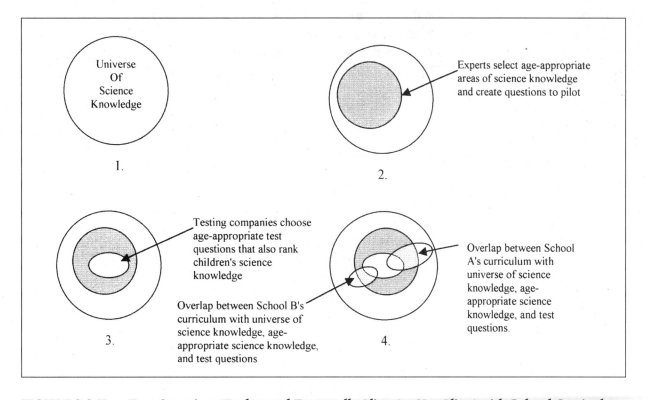

FIGURE 2.2 How Test Questions Evolve and Eventually Align (or Not Align) with School Curriculum

Creating comparison scores

> Sometimes a 33 is really a 40 . . .

After test creators select the items, they combine them to create a new test. Then they administer this test to a group of children who are intended to represent those who will eventually take the test. To create this *norm group*, test companies solicit the participation of schools from various geographic locations and socioeconomic levels. The sampling procedure carefully considers characteristics of children such as gender, ethnicity, age, and ability. Depending upon the company's financial resources, the norm group can be and should be quite large, numbering in the hundreds of thousands.

The text companies convert *raw scores* of the norm group to *standard scores* such as percentiles, stanines, normal curve equivalents, and grade equivalents. A raw score is the actual number of items correct. Because each subtest on a norm-referenced test may have a different number of items, raw scores are not useful in making comparisons. Standard scores permit comparisons.

Once test companies derive the standard scores, they use the scores to determine which standard score represents the raw scores of subsequent test-takers. For example, if a raw score of 33 in the norm group were converted to a percentile rank of 40, any child earning a raw score of 33 would be informed that her performance was equivalent to the fortieth percentile. Conversion of the norm group's raw scores to standard scores utilizes mathematical processes based on the concept of normal distribution. These calculations are beyond the scope of this book, but can be found in any statistics textbook.

Numbers and knowing

> Not everything that counts can be counted; not everything that can be counted, counts.
> *Albert Einstein*

What do norm-referenced scores tell you about what your students "know"? How can these scores inform your teaching? We will practically stand on our heads to underscore these next two points.

1. Your students' knowledge and scores are *relative* to the knowledge and scores of children in the norm group.
2. The knowledge reflected by the test *may or may not* adequately represent what your students know.

Test companies report standard scores, such as national percentiles, for each subtest. They may also supply state and local comparisons. In each instance, there is a norm group, be it national, state, or local, against which they compare your students.

A common misconception about national percentiles is that they represent a comparison of your students to all children of the same grade level. Some interpretive reports supplied by test companies perpetuate this misconception by making statements such as, "Your child scored higher than 80 percent of all fourth-grade students in the nation in social studies." However, you can see from the explanation above that this statement is misleading. It would be more accurate to say, "Your child scored higher than 80 percent of all fourth-grade students who were part of the national norm group." In other words, test companies compare the performance of your students only to the performance of students in the national norm group when they use national percentiles. *Your students' knowledge and scores are relative to the knowledge and scores of children in the norm group.*

Furthermore, the scores your students receive may not be accurate measures of their knowledge. For example, imagine that a student scored at the ninety-ninth percentile on the reading comprehension subtest, but received a "needs improvement" in reading on her report card. Or, think about a student who scored at the thirty-third percentile in spelling, yet consistently earned A's and B's on spelling tests. Mismatches like these between test scores and the classroom teacher's assessments of students' abilities confuse parents and sometimes put teachers in the difficult position of defending their evaluations in the face of seemingly contradictory evidence. So what's going on? *The knowledge reflected by the test may or may not adequately represent what your students know.*

The body of knowledge represented on the test may be inconsistent with the curriculum content and learning processes taught in the classroom. Remember that the test companies select items that represent a

FIGURE 2.3 NOT a "Norm" Group

field of knowledge, and those items must rank children's performances on the test. Your curriculum may address some of that knowledge, but not all. Further, your students may be learning very important concepts that are not represented on the tests. A child could know a great deal about a subject and still receive a relatively low score. Conversely, a child could be performing poorly in your classroom and receive a relatively high test score.

It would be easy at this point to take the high road and dismiss inconsistencies between students' test scores and classroom performances as irrelevant or as a fault of the test. However, national, norm-referenced tests represent a national curriculum and a set of expectations valued by the public. Scores on these tests often determine the educational opportunities available to your students. To be an effective advocate for your students, you need to paint as complete a picture of their abilities as you can. Information drawn from many different kinds of assessments, including norm-referenced tests, can help you meet their needs.

When you interpret test reports, remember:

1. Your students' knowledge and scores are relative to the knowledge and scores of children in the norm group.
2. The knowledge reflected by the test may or may not adequately represent what your students know.

Confirming and correcting your test answers

The answers to items 1–5 are as follows: 1. D, 2. B, 3. B, 4. C, and 5. B. (Give yourself partial credit if you selected some of our tongue-in-cheek responses.) Return to the beginning of this section and see if these answers make sense to you. If not, you might want to review the "Making Sense of Norms" section before proceeding with the chapter.

Section Two: Making Sense of Averages

Assessing Your Current Knowledge

Please respond to items 6 through 10. Choose the best response.

Use the following scores to answer items 6 and 8.
Class A test scores: 3, 4, 4, 5, 5, 5, 5, 6, 6, 7
Class B test scores: 0, 1, 2, 4, 5, 5, 6, 8, 9, 10

6. The mean for class A is
    A. larger than the mean for class B.
    B. the same as the mean for class B.
    C. smaller than the mean for class B.
    D. Don't have a clue.

7. The mean and median are both types of averages. They are also called measures of central tendency. The median is the score that falls in the middle of a group of scores. If a student scored at the median on a norm-referenced test, the only serious statement we could *not* make is that she
   A. scored at the mean.
   B. attained an average score.
   C. got about half the items correct.
   D. scored at the fiftieth percentile.
   E. took her test sitting on the grassy strip in the middle of the interstate (it could happen!).

8. The standard deviation reflects the variability of the scores. Based on your analysis of the scores, the standard deviation for class A is
   A. larger than the standard deviation for class B.
   B. the same as the standard deviation for class B.
   C. smaller than the standard deviation for class B.
   D. Don't really care what the standard deviation is.

Read this passage to answer item nine.

The headline in the local paper read, "Test Scores Hover Near Average." The article reported performance on a norm-referenced test and stated that statewide, the median percentile for high school students was just above the fiftieth percentile. The state superintendent was quoted to have said, "Average performance is not our goal for our children. Average performance is not adequate today and will be even less adequate in the future."

9. The spirit of the state superintendent's message is clear. Her goal is admirable, but complicated by the statistical nature of norm-referenced tests. Which of the following statements is/are accurate?
   A. Only in Lake Wobegon[1] are all children above average.
   B. Even if the median percentile were to rise to 60 or 70, half the students would still fall below that percentile—below average.

[1]Lake Wobegon won a place in American culture when Garrison Keillor, author of the radio broadcast, *Prairie Home Companion*, characterized a fictitious Lake Wobegon as a place where "all the men are strong, all the women are good looking, and all the children are above average." We thought everyone knew that, until some of our younger (humph!) colleagues and students alerted us that the reference meant nothing to them. We continue to use this item because this is a good example of a *distracter* in a multiple-choice response. Although the cultural context is not needed to answer the question, it may distract the reader from the substance of the response.

C. If over time schools in the state were to build their curriculum around the knowledge represented in the test items, and the test was not renormed, it would be possible for all students to be above the fiftieth percentile.

D. All of the above.

10. The scoring scale for the SAT was created in 1941, based on the performance of a norm group of test-takers. The scores formed a normal curve with an average (or mean) score of 500. However, by 1993, the mean for students taking the verbal section of the SAT was 424, and the mean for the math section was 478. As a result, the scoring scale for the SAT was "recentered" in 1994, again with an average score of 500. Based on this information, which of the following statements is/are accurate?

A. A student who had a 424 for the verbal section of the SAT in 1993 would have had a score of 500 after the SAT was recentered.

B. In 1993, a student scoring 424 on the verbal and 478 on the math could conclude that he or she had a stronger ability in math.

C. A student scoring 478 on the math in 1993 and a student scoring 500 on the math after the scale was recentered would each have been at the fiftieth percentile.

D. All of the above.

E. A & C but not B.

F. A & B but not C.

G. B & C but not A.

H. I hate multiple-choice questions!

Expanding Your Understanding of Averages

By understanding norm groups and the relationship between raw scores and standard scores such as percentiles, you could probably give an adequate explanation of an individual student's scores. However, to explain the relationship between a student's scores and an "average," and to adequately interpret the meaning of test scores that represent the performance of groups of students, you need to understand two more key concepts: *normal distribution* and *averages*. Are you ready to take a quick slide down the normal curve? As you slip along, look for these major ideas:

1. Norm-referenced tests are based on the assumption that academic achievement is normally distributed.

2. What is considered "average" depends on which statistical definition is being used.

3. Your students' performances may vary widely but still be described as "average" on a test report.

4. Median scores have limitations as comparative tools and should be interpreted cautiously.

FIGURE 2.4 Sliding Down the "Norm"-al Curve

Perhaps one of the most misunderstood concepts in testing is the "average," a term used frequently in our culture. We hear people talk about average height and weight, average family income, the average family, batting averages, or an average student. We worry if our cholesterol is above average, yet celebrate when our children's SAT scores are described the same way. In short, we bring a mixed bag of definitions and reactions to things we call average.

So, what does average mean? It depends. To understand one way test companies use the concept in norm-referenced testing, you must first tackle normal distribution.

Average and the normal distribution

> "When I use a word," Humpty Dumpty said, in rather a scornful tone, "it means just what I choose it to mean—neither more nor less."
>
> "The question is," said Alice, "whether you can make words mean so many different things."
>
> *Lewis Carroll,* Through the Looking Glass

The world of testing seems to agree with Humpty Dumpty. In this domain, words are used to mean something quite particular, nothing more and nothing less. When reports discuss normal distribution, "normal" does not mean the same thing as "Her behavior was normal" or "It was a normal day." Rather, "normal distribution" refers to the *shape* created when we graph numbers representing various natural phenomena. The mathematical properties of this distribution are used to predict how frequently certain characteristics will occur.

Figure 2.5 shows a line drawing of a graph that visually represents a normal distribution.

What do you notice about this figure? It's shaped like a bell, it's symmetrical around a dotted line, and there is more space under the "hump" than at either end. This shape is created when we graph numbers representing characteristics such as height, weight, intelligence, or achievement. (These are just a few examples; this shape represents many characteristics found in nature.) The dotted line represents a middle point. The differences in the amount of space under the curved line occur because for any characteristic, there are fewer cases at the extremes than in the middle. The majority of cases will fall under the "hump" and will disperse symmetrically around that middle point.

Although many people can readily accept that characteristics like height and weight are distributed in the way the bell-shaped curve suggests, they may have a more difficult time accepting that characteristics like intelligence and achievement, *as expressed by test scores*, are also normally distributed. However, this assumption is fundamental to the development of a norm-referenced test and its interpretation. In short, *norm-referenced tests are based on the assumption that academic achievement is normally distributed.*[2]

Because norm-referenced tests are based on the concept of normal distribution, test-makers must select items that will result in a normal distribution of performance. Companies construct tests to increase

FIGURE 2.5 The "Norm"-al Distribution

[2]One unfortunate interpretation of this theory is the claim that certain populations can be *a priori* assigned a particular place on the normal distribution. This interpretation is inaccurate.

the likelihood that some children will perform poorly, some will perform extremely well, and most will perform in a mid or average range. If test scores of a norm group were graphed, they would result in a bell-shaped curve. Some test reports describe scores falling in the area under the "hump" as average performance. Those at the extremes would be above or below average.

Other uses of average

> If you have one hand on the stove, and the other on the refrigerator, on average you're comfortable . . .

We've just described one way to use the term "average"—as a range of scores that fall in a particular area under the normal curve. Another way to describe average performance is to think about where the central point is among a group of scores. Two types of averages, mean and median, represent the central points of a group of norm-referenced test scores. Where is the central point? Well, it depends on whether companies report the mean or the median. In other words, *what is considered "average" depends on which statistical definition is being used.*

Mean   A *mean* is the figure most of us think about when we hear the question, "What is the average of this group of numbers?" To calculate the mean, sum a group of scores and divide the sum by the total number of scores. For example: 1 + 1 + 3 + 50 + 250 = 305. The sum, 305, divided by 5 (the number of scores) is 61, the mean. Note that when you calculate the mean, every score, including those at the extremes, will affect its value.

Companies construct norm-referenced tests to equate the mean score with the fiftieth percentile. This discrete number then becomes a dividing point for describing scores as either "above average" (above the mean) or "below average" (below the mean). This definition generally makes everyone feel comfortable that they know what they are talking about.

But. (You knew there would be a "but.")

You will seldom see the mean used to report your students' individual scores. The mean plays its most important role in helping to determine the range of scores that fall under the "hump" of the normal curve. By definition, 68 percent of the scores of children in the norm group will fall in this area (see Figure 2.6). The test companies use the *mean* and a statistic called the *standard deviation* to calculate which scores will fall in this range. The mean (fiftieth percentile) identifies a central point in a group of scores and the standard deviation describes how the scores spread out around that central point. For example, on one widely used intelligence test, the mean is equated to a score of 100 and the standard deviation is fifteen points. A score of 85 is then one standard deviation below the mean (100 minus 15) and a score of 115 is one standard deviation above the mean (100 plus 15). Sixty-eight percent of people's scores on that test fall between 85 and 115. Because the mean and standard deviation vary from test to test, *the scores that fall under the "hump" of the normal curve will vary.*

When we define "average" performance in this way, scores that range from the fifteenth to the eighty-fifth percentiles are within the average range. *Your students' performances may vary widely but still be described as "average" on a test report.* Therefore, you may need to adjust your concept of average when you interpret norm-referenced test reports. Test reports rarely portray this information in the form of a bell-shaped curve. Rather, you are more likely to see a chart with the average range shaded like the one in Figure 2.7.

Median   A *median* is the score that falls in the middle of a group of scores, with an equal number of scores above and below it. For example:

Scores: 1, 1, 3, 50, 250
Scores: 1, 1, 3, 4, 5

In both sets, the score of 3 is the median. Unlike the mean, which is affected by the value of every score, the median is affected only by the number of scores and not by their values.

Test reports frequently use the median to represent the performance of groups of students, usually at the classroom, school, or district levels. When reports give median percentile scores, those scores simply mean that half of the scores (of students in your classroom, school, district, etc.) were higher, and half were lower. Since the

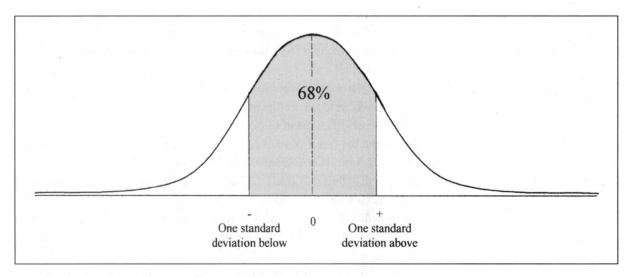

FIGURE 2.6 One Definition of Average

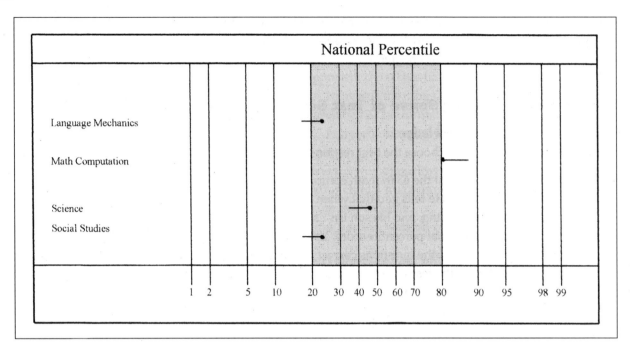

FIGURE 2.7 Sample Test Report with Average Scores

median says nothing about the value of the scores, you have no idea how high or how low those scores were.

In other words, a median percentile score of 50 could mean that all the scores above the median were at the ninetieth percentile and all the scores below clustered between the fortieth and fiftieth percentiles. Or it could mean that the scores above the median ranged from the fifty-first to the ninety-ninth percentiles, while the scores below the median clustered between the tenth and twentieth percentiles. Or it could mean some other configuration of scores; you simply don't know. From these scenarios, it is easy to see *median scores have limitations as comparative tools and should be interpreted cautiously.*

When you interpret test reports, remember:

1. Norm-referenced tests are based on the assumption that academic achievement is normally distributed.
2. What is considered "average" depends on which statistical definition is being used.
3. Your students' performances may vary widely but still be described as "average" on a test report.
4. Median scores have limitations as comparative tools and should be interpreted cautiously.

Confirming and correcting your test answers

The answers to items 6–10 are as follows: 6. B, 7. C, 8. C, 9. D, and 10. E. (If you knew about Lake Wobegon, give yourself extra credit.) Return

instance, if one of your students received a percentile score of 43, you would tell her parents, "Your daughter scored at the forty-third percentile, which means that she scored better than 43 percent of the students in the norm group." Or, you might say, "Your daughter's percentile rank was 43, which means that she scored better than 43 percent of the students in the norm group."

There are also ways you should *not* describe percentiles because you risk conveying inaccurate or misleading information. You should not say, "Your daughter's percentile score of 43 means she got 43 percent of the items correct." This statement would reinforce a common misperception that a percentile is the percentage of items a student answered correctly. *It is not.* Nor should you say, "Your daughter scored better than 43 percent of all the children at her grade level in the nation." As pervasive as norm-referenced tests may seem, it is simply not true that all of the children in the nation at any grade level have taken a particular test. Comparisons can be made *only* to the norm group—period.

Now that we have all *that* squared away, let's talk about another way percentiles are misused. We shudder to mention it, but do you know that some people try to average percentiles? We know they're well intentioned, but *they truly don't know what they mean* (so to speak). Here's why. We cannot average percentiles because they represent unequal measuring units. Put another way, the distance between percentile ranks on the normal curve is not the same. See for yourself. Look at the placement of percentile ranks on the normal curve below. Notice that the distance between the percentile ranks of 10 and 20 is different than the distance between the percentile ranks of 50 and 60. Trying to average percentile ranks would be like trying to average one

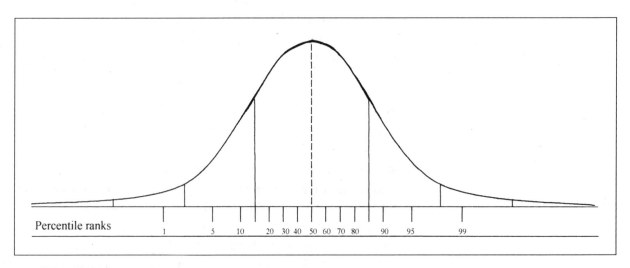

FIGURE 2.8 Normal Curve and Percentile Ranks

number measured in centimeters and a second number measured in inches. Unless you convert the numbers to equalize the measurement (e.g., convert inches to centimeters), the calculation is meaningless.

Connecting percentiles and normal curve equivalents For this reason, people sometimes translate scores into normal curve equivalents. Normal curve equivalents (NCEs) divide the normal curve into ninety-nine equal intervals. Each NCE is equivalent to a percentile rank. For instance, an NCE of 58.1 is equal to a percentile rank of 65. You don't need to know how to convert NCEs into percentile ranks; readily available charts list these for you. *NCEs can be averaged and, unlike percentiles, they can be used to compare scores of groups of students across tests.*

Now here's the tricky part. Sometimes reports will list scores as mean percentiles. Wait a minute! Didn't we just say that you could never average percentiles?

Well, you can't. But you can average NCEs. If your district administrators were talking about a mean percentile, they were probably talking about the percentile rank that was equivalent to the average NCE score. On the other hand, watch out for sloppy translations. One local paper listed the "average" test scores over a seven-year period by school. When we called to find out what those figures represented, we were told that the reporter had taken the national percentile ranks for each school and averaged them. If you encounter similar information, you will know that the calculation is inappropriate, and that the numbers are misleading and inaccurate.

Percentiles and confidence intervals

Imagine you are taking the same test over and over, but you had no opportunity to learn anything new between each testing session and you recall nothing about the test from the time before. Would you expect to obtain the same score each time? Of course not. No test is perfectly constructed, and a variety of factors would affect you each time you took the test—motivation, memory, fatigue, and emotions, to name a few. However, if it were possible to take a test an infinite number of times, your scores would form a normal distribution. The mean of that distribution would be your true score.

We can never know when a person takes a test what her true score is. The best we can do is use a statistic called the standard error of measurement to estimate the range of scores within which a person's true score would fall. This range is called a confidence interval. The interpretive reports of students' test scores provided by the testing companies often include a chart that shows the *obtained score* (the score reported) as a dot bracketed by lines extending to the left and right. Rather than thinking of a student as scoring at a single percentile, you would find the percentile ranks at the lower and upper ends of the lines and conclude more accurately that the student's true score fell somewhere between those two percentiles (see the chart below).

Understanding confidence intervals is crucial since so many educational decisions are made on single, discrete scores. For example, your district might admit students to special programs if their test scores were at or above (or below) a particular percentile rank. If scores were interpreted using the more accurate confidence intervals, more students would have access to those services.

Percentiles and taking tests

When does understanding the implications of percentiles benefit your students and your school? Always. Understanding percentiles has far deeper implications than merely increasing your effectiveness in translating the meaning of scores. *For all practical purposes, students whose scores fall at the mid or average percentile range can more easily increase their percentile ranks by answering a few more test items correctly than students whose scores fall at the upper and lower ends.* It is not as easy for students whose scores fall at the upper and lower ends of the curve to increase their scores. Why? Because percentiles are not spread out evenly over the normal curve. They bunch together more closely toward the middle of the curve than they do at either end of the curve. Since by definition, the majority (68 percent) of scores fall in the mid-range, a substantial

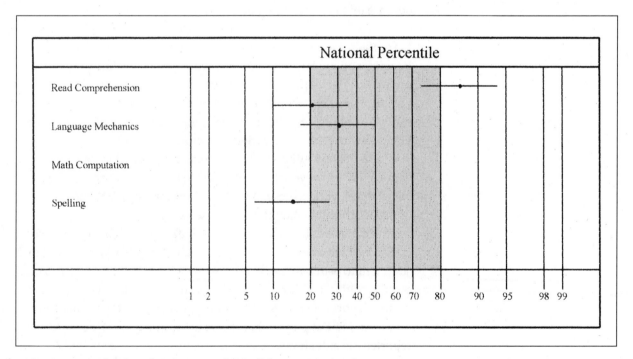

FIGURE 2.9 Obtained Scores and Confidence Intervals

number of your students may be able to increase their percentile ranks by improving their ability to demonstrate their knowledge on norm-referenced tests.

For individual students, scoring higher on the test may open more educational opportunities, and may have a positive impact on their attitudes toward tests and on perceptions of their abilities. As you recall from Chapter One, repeated, negative experiences with norm-referenced tests have a cumulative negative impact on students' performance. Politically, higher percentile rankings for your school will mean that the public perceives the school more positively as a place where learning is occurring, teaching is effective, and public funds are being used well. Lower percentile rankings do not necessarily mean that learning is inadequate or teaching is ineffective. However, political decisions made about schools often reflect public perceptions, and these decisions may affect the choices you can make about curriculum and approaches to teaching and learning.

Whether or not you feel you can make good use of norm-referenced test scores, ignoring their power is perilous both for your students and for you as an educator. State legislators use norm-referenced test scores as a rationale for introducing bills that dictate to professional educators the curricula and methodology they must use. For example, legislation has been introduced in Washington and Arizona to require "scientifically valid" approaches to reading instruction. This trend is disturbing, and can be countered in part by helping children demonstrate what they know and can do on norm-referenced tests.

Stanines

This section on stanines is brief because stanines, although sometimes included in test reports, are not used as often as percentiles and NCEs. We want to offer a definition and provide a little information about what this type of score means, just in case you need to know. Stanine is short for "standard score of nine units." Test companies report stanines in single-digit values from 1 through 9. Interestingly, stanines were developed during World War II in part as an efficiency measure. By using single-digit numbers to represent a score that fell within a certain range of values, more scores could be recorded on IBM key-punch cards, the cutting edge of technology in those days. Stanines are similar to normal curve equivalents because they divide the normal curve into equal measuring units. Instead of the NCE's ninety-nine equal intervals, stanines divide the curve into nine equal units, and for this reason they can be used to compare performance across subtests. If reports use stanines, average scores would be stanines 4, 5, or 6.

Grade equivalents

The best advice we can give about grade equivalent scores is this: Don't use them. Just say no. They are confusing, misleading, and extremely difficult to explain. The term "grade equivalent" suggests a clear relationship between student ability and grade level that simply does not exist. That said, here's what grade equivalent scores are not. If a child in third grade receives a grade equivalent score of 5.1 on a reading subtest, it does *not* mean that child has mastered all the reading skills taught by the first month of fifth grade. It does *not* mean that the child has the skills to do fifth-grade work in reading. It does *not* mean the child would do well in fifth-grade reading. It does *not* mean that the child should be promoted to fifth grade. And it does *not* mean that the child understood the reading skills covered by the test about as well as an average fifth-grader.

It does mean that the student's raw score on the reading test was the same as the average score of students at the beginning of fifth grade in the norm group who took the same test. Yes, you understood that correctly. Third- and fifth-graders would have taken the same test in order for the test company to establish the comparative scores. To further complicate matters, companies do not base every grade equivalent score on the actual performance of students at different grade levels. Rather, they estimate many of the grade equivalent scores based on trends in the test scores of the norm group.

When you interpret test reports, remember:

1. A percentile score will tell you what percentage of students in the norm group scored at or below the raw score of one of your students.
2. NCEs can be averaged and, unlike percentiles, they can be used to compare scores of groups of students across tests.
3. For all practical purposes, students whose scores fall at the mid or average percentile range can more easily increase their percentile ranks by answering a few more test items correctly than students whose scores fall at the upper and lower ends.
4. It is more accurate to interpret a student's test performance using the range of scores identified by the confidence intervals than by using one fixed score.
5. Grade equivalents are misleading and should be avoided if possible.

Confirming and correcting your test answers

The answers to items 11–14 are as follows: 11. C, 12. D, 13. D, 14. A. (Give yourself five extra points if you don't use grade equivalent scores!) Return to the beginning of this section and see if these answers make sense to you. If not, you might want to review the "Making Sense of Test Scores" section before proceeding to the next chapter.

CHAPTER THREE

When Parents Meet "Norm"

Helping Parents Understand Test Scores

Now that we've reviewed how companies construct tests and what the scores mean, it's time to consider how to convey this information effectively to parents. After all, they don't know "Norm" like you do. This chapter explores constructive ways to help parents understand Norm. You'll find a discussion of a general framework you can use to help structure conversations with parents about tests. Using this framework, we model possible responses to typical parents' questions. We've concluded the chapter with a "cheat sheet" of terms and definitions that can serve as a quick reference.

FIGURE 3.1 DILBERT *reprinted by permission of United Feature Syndicate, Inc.*

Self-Assessment

Think about how you would respond to the parents who raised the questions that follow. Take a moment to jot down replies that would help parents make sense of the test scores and gain a greater understanding of how well children are learning. Keep in mind that the following general responses, though tempting, are not likely to do the trick when parents meet Norm.

- Don't worry about those test scores; they don't mean anything.
- Our school counselor will be happy to talk with you.
- Everything's great; your child/school is doing fine.
- Beats me. What do you think?

Parents' Questions

My son is smart! He's been helping me in the shop since he was five. How could he fail math computation? He only got a 63. And what's this stanine thing?

According to this paper, my daughter has mastered all the reading skills measured by the reading test. It says she scored higher than 99 percent of the fourth-grade children in the whole country. That's pretty great, isn't it? So, why did she get a "needs improvement" in reading from you on her last report card? Why isn't she in the accelerated reading program?

Looks like my son isn't doing too great in spelling. His score was only 33. Does that mean he has a learning disability? Why has he been getting A's and B's on his spelling tests? What can I do to help him?

My daughter scored at the third-grade level in language mechanics, but she's a fourth-grader! This report says she needs work on adjectives and adverbs. What does this mean? We insist that our children speak properly. She uses adjectives and adverbs in her writing. What are you going to do about this?

I've been living in this section of town for five years and I am really tired of seeing our neighborhood school reported in the paper as having one of the lowest average test scores in the district. Can you please help me understand what's going on?

We moved into this neighborhood because we were told this school had the highest test scores in town. That's been true for the two years our son has been here. Now we see in the newspaper that another school has higher scores. What's going on?

A Framework for Talking with Parents

Teachers talk with parents and community members about tests and test scores in a variety of situations, ranging from formal conferences to chance encounters in the grocery store. Wherever the conversation takes place, we have found it useful to follow a general framework of response. This framework speaks to three concerns: the importance of (1) acknowledging interests and emotions, (2) using nontechnical language to explain test concepts, and (3) connecting test performance with other classroom assessments and school curricula. In each of these areas, our goal is to help teachers and parents work as partners. When teachers provide information accurately and in nondefensive ways, the potential for partnership increases.

Acknowledging Interests and Emotions

Perception is tricky. In every new encounter, approximately 80 percent of what we "see" is shaped by our prior experiences. Every time parents and teachers meet, they bring with them memories of past encounters that affect their current perceptions. Experiences with taking tests, being judged by tests, and talking about tests affect parent-teacher communication. It is essential to be aware that the interests and emotions associated with this implicit foundation will affect conversations about children and their educational needs. In other words, you have your own baggage, and parents have theirs.

Because prior experiences influence perception, emotions about test scores often run high for both parents and teachers and color their interactions. Sometimes these emotions will be a subtle undercurrent to conversation; other times they will be overt, strong, and impossible to avoid. In either case, particpants need to acknowledge these emotions or the conversation won't move to a place where teachers and parents can discuss the best interests of children.

Before talking with parents about norm-referenced tests, teachers need to acknowledge to themselves their own interests or concerns. They may want to ask themselves:

■ What's my position on state-mandated achievement tests?
■ Do I believe this type of test tells me anything about what my students know?
■ Am I confident I have enough information to interpret test scores adequately?
■ Do I feel pressured to raise test scores?
■ Am I worried that parents will judge my teaching by the test scores?
■ Do I plan to use the test scores to persuade parents to pursue a particular course of action?
■ Am I afraid of parents' emotional reactions to the scores?

Whatever the concerns or interests of the teacher may be, he needs to take care that he is able to hear what the parents actually want to know. A few moments of self-reflection may improve parent-teacher communication.

Teachers facilitate this communication when they acknowledge parent concerns or particular interests. Parents may be worried, angry, confused, or jubilant. Or, they may simply be intent on gathering or clarifying information. Parents may see themselves as advocates for their children, either in partnership with the teachers or as defenders of their children's rights and needs. Some parents may feel powerless to influence their child's school experiences, and will approach conferences with resignation or deference to the teacher's judgments. However parents may feel, teachers can begin to establish a climate of trust and collaboration by demonstrating that they recognize the parents' interests or concerns.

Using Nontechnical Language to Explain Test Concepts

It's probably safe to say that very few people have a background in statistics and test construction. Yet, test reports are couched in language derived from statistical theory and are often confusing and difficult to understand. Parents need to know what norm-referenced test scores mean, and they expect teachers to provide that information. The second part of our framework for talking with parents about tests emphasizes communicating in accessible, nontechnical language. Chapter Two and the "cheat sheet" at the end of this chapter should help teachers translate test terms into plain language.

Connecting Test Performance with Other Assessments and School Curricula

The third part of this framework emphasizes the importance of connecting performance on the test with classroom curriculum and the variety of other assessments used to complete the profile of a child's knowledge. To address this third area, teachers need to answer the following questions:

1. Do the test scores and the interpretive remarks on the test report confirm your understanding of the students' knowledge in a particular subject area? If so, point out this relationship to the parents and use the student's classroom work to confirm areas of strength and areas that need more development.
2. Do the test scores and interpretive remarks challenge your understanding of a students' knowledge in a particular subject area? If so, ask yourself:

- Are there trends or patterns in the performance of your class that suggest that there are shared areas of strength and shared gaps in knowledge?
- If there are gaps, can you account for these because the knowledge or skills are not part of your local curriculum or have not yet been addressed in class?

Your analysis is important and will help parents understand apparent discrepancies between norm-referenced test scores and progress reports from class. You might also reassure parents by talking about your plans for addressing gaps in knowledge and skills or by explaining the reasons why you will not cover those areas. For example, in one district that we know, the spelling scores on the state norm-referenced test are quite low. However, to improve the scores substantially, the district would need to change the content and approach of its spelling program. At this point, the district has chosen not to make these changes. They have concluded that there is sufficient evidence other than test scores to demonstrate that children in the district are learning to spell.

Modeling the Framework: Suggested Responses to Parent Questions

We used the three steps of our framework to construct the following responses. As you read them, look for ways in which we acknowledged interests and emotions, communicated test scores and concepts in nontechnical language, and connected the test scores with other assessments and school curricula.

My son is smart! He's been helping me in the shop since he was five. How could he fail math computation? He only got a 63. And what's this stanine thing?

I understand why this score is confusing. Most of us would think of a 63 as an F, based on our experiences of school grading systems. In those systems, a 63 means that you only got 63 percent of the items correct. I assure you that's not what this score means. This is a percentile, not a percentage. Your son scored at the sixty-third percentile, which means he scored higher than sixty-three percent of the students in the norm group. Let me explain what a norm group is. When the test companies develop tests, they select a group of students who represent all the kids who may eventually take this test. Your son's score was compared to theirs. Another way to say all this is your son scored better than almost two-thirds of the students in the norm group.

The stanine score that you are pointing out is another type of score used to compare your son's performance to the norm group. There are nine stanines and stanine scores of 4, 5, and 6 are considered average. Your son's performance fell in the fifth stanine.

So what do the scores mean? One score suggests he performed "above average" on the test and the other suggests his performance was average. To understand more clearly how your son is doing in math, we need to look at the work in his math portfolio. Let me tell you about the types of math we've been working on and show you some of your son's work. (Then address any discrepancies between the math skills assessed on the norm-referenced test and the math skills taught in your district for the age group of the student.)

According to this paper, my daughter has mastered all the reading skills measured by the reading test. It says she scored higher than 99 percent of the fourth-grade children in the whole country. That's pretty great, isn't it? So, why did she get a "needs improvement" in reading from you on her last report card? Why isn't she in the accelerated reading program?

Your daughter did really well on the test. She scored higher than 99 percent of the fourth-grade students in the norm group. I'm sure you're proud of her, and I understand why you seem concerned about her last report card.

There are definite differences between the way the norm-referenced test assesses reading and the way I assess reading in the classroom. Each assessment method has a different set of expectations and requires a different set of skills. The test uses a multiple-choice format to measure children's abilities to select facts, conclusions, and opinions from a set of options. This format seems to work well for your daughter.

(What follows is an attempt to illustrate differences in classroom-based and norm-referenced assessments. The details would, of course, differ by classroom.)

In our class, I assess comprehension by having the children write about and discuss the characters, events, and themes of the stories. As you can see from your daughter's journal, she provides very little information about the characters or about her understanding of themes. I've also noticed that she almost never talks during group discussions. That's why her report card said "needs improvement." It's wonderful that your daughter can select correct answers on a test, but I also want her to develop her ability to talk and write about what she sees as important in the stories.

On the other hand, I recognize that I need to use different types of assessments to measure children's progress. Since your daughter seems to do well on multiple-choice tests, I would be willing to use them occasionally. I want to be sure she remains confident about herself as a reader as she learns new ways to show her understanding of the reading materials.

Looks like my son isn't doing too great in spelling. His score was only 33. Does that mean he has a learning disability? Why has he been getting A's and B's on his spelling tests? What can I do to help him?

It is confusing, isn't it? Your son has been doing very well on our spelling tests using the district spelling list and the theme lists we create in class. And I hear your concern about the learning disability, but I don't think there's anything here to suggest he has one. None of his classwork indicates that he has a learning disability, and norm-referenced tests are not designed to diagnose learning disabilities. Let me explain what his score means and then I'll tell you what I think may be happening.

This type of test is called a norm-referenced test, which means that every child's score is compared to the scores of a norm group. When the test companies develop tests, they select a group of students who are intended to represent all the kids who may eventually take this test. Your son's score was compared to theirs. He scored at the thirty-third percentile, which means he scored higher than 33 percent of the kids in the norm group.

You're right that the thirty-third percentile doesn't seem to represent your child's abilities in spelling. There may be several reasons for that. My guess is that the way the spelling words were presented on the test was confusing. On the test, kids don't actually spell the words like they do in class. Instead, they have to choose the correct spelling from among several variations. Some kids find this easy; others don't. However, the ability to choose a correctly spelled word from among several similar variations is not the same as spelling words as you're writing. As you can see from his classwork, your son is quite capable of correctly spelling many words from our themes and from the district list. He is also conscientious about editing his work for spelling before he hands it in.

My daughter scored at the third-grade level in language mechanics, but she's a fourth-grader! This report says she needs work on adjectives and adverbs. What does this mean? We insist that our children speak properly. She uses adjectives and adverbs in her writing. What are you going to do about this?

You're right—your daughter uses descriptive words both when she's talking and when she's writing. I can see you're upset about seeing her work described as being at the third-grade level. Let me explain a little more about the test language and about what the test is measuring in this section.

The score you're questioning is a grade equivalent score. Grade equivalents are one of many types of standard scores reported by test companies. All standard scores compare your child's performance with the performance of children in a norm group. The norm group is intended to be representative of kids who take the test.

A grade equivalent of 3.1 does not mean that your daughter is doing third-grade work. What it means is that she did not perform on the test at the level the test company would predict for fourth-graders. However, my assessment is that she is using language at a level that I would expect for fourth-graders, so let's explore several alternative explanations.

When I see an inconsistency like this, at least two possibilities come to mind. The first explanation I'd consider would focus on your daughter and her experience of the test. I'd think about different factors: Was she tired when she took this section? Did she work quickly enough to get through the test? Was she distracted by questions she couldn't answer? Did she lose her place on the answer sheet? You see what I'm getting at—there could be many reasons why your daughter performed poorly on this section and none of them have much to do with what she knows.

The second explanation I'd consider is the content and format of the test itself. Is there a match between what we teach and what the test measures, and how we teach and how the test measures knowledge? It's very possible that the test may be asking children to demonstrate knowledge that we haven't taught them yet, or in a way that is foreign to them.

In this case, I'd have to talk to your daughter to know what this section of the test was like for her. As for the match between the curriculum of our school and the curriculum of the test, well, writing is a complex process that involves many different skills. Language mechanics—the ability to use language conventionally—is just one of them, and there is no agreement nationally about when those skills should be introduced. For instance, in our curriculum, children write a great deal, but we don't spend much time teaching the labels of language. Your daughter can use adjectives and adverbs, but she may not know how to label words with these terms.

I'm not sure what explanations make sense for your daughter, but I'm going to look over the scores of all the children in the class and see if any patterns emerge.

I've been living in this section of town for five years and I am really tired of seeing our neighborhood school reported in the paper as having one of the lowest average test scores in the district. Can you please help me understand what's going on?

I know how discouraging it is to see low test scores reported year after year. I've been teaching here for ten years and I am certain we're helping children learn. There are good reasons why the test scores reported in the paper do not adequately represent what all the children in this school know. I'd have to check, but usually the paper reports median percentile scores. This score means that half of the children in the school scored below this point and half scored above. So we do have many children scoring quite high on the test, but you can't tell that from the newspaper. We also have children who do not score well. Here are some of the reasons children at our school receive low scores.

(Note: There are many reasons for low test scores that could be discussed straightforwardly at this point. We think these are some of the most common. Some schools experience a poor match between the test and their curriculum content. Others have a high population of ESL students who may be very knowledgeable but unable to express their knowledge in English. In some schools, teachers and parents are vocal in expressing negative attitudes towards tests, which may influence children's motivation. Negative or indifferent attitudes of parents towards education may be an issue. Scores may be low if there is a consistent mismatch between teaching approaches and children's needs. Finally, inadequate or inequitable distribution of funding and support may impact students' opportunities to learn and, thus, their performances on tests.)

Let me tell you about some of the ways we are trying to address the challenges we're facing.

We moved into this neighborhood because we were told this school had the highest test scores in town. That's been true for the two years our son has been here. Now we see in the newspaper that another school has higher scores. What's going on?

Option One: Drop in your school's test scores is minimal.

Sounds like you're kind of puzzled by what's going on. Our test scores did drop a couple of points. They are a bit lower than the scores of the school you're referring to. It's not unusual for these types of scores to fluctuate. If there had been a big change, or if this was part of a pattern that had been developing over a number of years, there could be cause for concern. But a change of just a few points has more to do with the ways tests are constructed than with a change in the achievement of our students. We always use the test scores to evaluate our curriculum, and at this point we don't see any reason to be concerned. Please come out to the school if you can and we'll be happy to show you what we've been doing.

Option Two: Drop in your school's test scores is substantial (more than ten percentile points).

Sounds like you're worried and so am I. We always expect some fluctuation in test scores, but this much change has caused us to look carefully at what may be happening. I can't offer you conclusive answers right now, but here are some of the possibilities we're investigating. You probably realize that the scores we have this year are from a different group of children than last year. We're looking at how this year's kids compare to last year's. Sometimes a group, for whatever reason, is dramatically different from other groups. We're trying to see if that's what's happening here. (Note: Boundary changes, significant increases in the ESL population, or sheer chance may explain large differences in test scores attributable to the population of kids.)

Another possibility is our curriculum and how well it reflects what the test measures. We began piloting a new reading and math program three years ago. This is the first group of children who have taken the state test who were exposed only to this curriculum. We don't assume there's anything wrong with the curriculum because the test scores are lower. But we do need to look at the match between what we're teaching and what the test assesses. We should have information to share at a parent meeting within the next month.

Option Three: Your school's test scores stay the same; other school's scores increase substantially.

I noticed that, too, and started wondering about it. If the difference had been only a few points I would just assume it was ordinary fluctuation. But we're looking at a pretty big difference here, which suggests to me several different possibilities. They might have decided to use a systematic approach to test preparation. Or, their new curriculum may be more closely aligned with the test than their previous one. By that I mean there may be a closer match between the knowledge the test assesses and what the children are being taught. Another possibility is that the group of students they tested this year, for whatever reason, is very different from last year's group. Since our test scores are still high, and I have confidence in our curriculum, I'm not concerned about the difference between our test scores and theirs. But I am curious and want to look into it more.

Teachers' Cheat Sheet:
A Quick Reference of Common Test Terms

We discuss many of the following terms and concepts in Chapters Two and Three. We think this list might serve as a quick reference when you're talking with parents. These short, nontechnical definitions might help you expand your repertoire of stock replies to questions parents typically ask about tests.

Achievement Test Standardized test that measures knowledge and skills students have acquired in typical academic areas such as reading (vocabulary, word analysis, reading comprehension); language (spelling, mechanics, usage); mathematics (computation, concepts, applications); social studies; science; and study skills.

Battery A set of several tests designed to be given together as a unit.

Confidence Interval The *range* of scores within which a person's true score is likely to fall. No test score is without error; use of confidence intervals provides a more accurate estimate of a student's performance.

Constructed Response Test items that require students to write a short or extended (longer) answer.

Criterion-Referenced Tests Tests that compare a student's performance to a preset standard of acceptable performance rather than to the performance of other students. At their most basic, criterion-referenced test scores can be interpreted to mean, "Does he know it?" "Can she do it?", *not*, "Does he know it or can she do it better than someone else?"

Grade Equivalent (GE) A standard score that compares a student's score to scores across a number of grade levels. The usual *misinterpretation* of this score is that a student is performing in a manner equivalent to a particular grade level. However, what really happens is that test companies compute the average (mean) score of norm groups at each grade level. For instance, a grade equivalent score of 3.1 corresponds to the average score of students in the first month of third grade. A second-grade student with a grade equivalent score of 3.1 is not necessarily ready for third-grade work, because the performance is being measured on a test of second-grade content. Given the confusion of interpretation, *just say no* to the use of grade equivalent scores.

Mean A type of average indicating a central point in a group of scores. The test companies calculate mean by adding together a group of scores and dividing the sum by the number of scores. Because it is affected by the value of every score in the group, the mean may not be the best measure to use if there are very high or low scores that differ substantially from the majority of the scores.

Median A type of average that identifies the middle of a group of scores; half the scores are above the median and half the scores are below. The values of the scores do not affect the median.

Norm Group A group of children whose performance on the test becomes the standard against which test companies compare all other children's performances. The test companies intend the children in the norm group to represent the children who will eventually take the test.

Norm-Referenced Tests Tests that compare the performance of the test-taker to the performance of a pre-selected norm group.

Normal Curve A bell-shaped curve that represents the distribution of test scores. If the distribution is "normal," most scores will fall within an average range under the "hump" of the curve.

Normal Curve Equivalent (NCE) A standard score that represents one of ninety-nine equally spaced points on the normal curve. Each NCE corresponds to a percentile.

Obtained Score The score a student earns (obtains) on a given day. Test performance is always affected by error introduced by the test (there's no such thing as a perfect test) or by the test-taker (who may be tired, distracted, off-track on the bubble sheets, etc.). For this reason, if the student were to take the same test again, she might earn (obtain) a different score.

Percentage Correct Score Score that shows the test-taker's performance as a percentage of the maximum score possible. For example, if the maximum score possible is 50 and the student gets 30 answers correct, the percentage correct score is 60 percent ($30/50 \times 100 = 60\%$). Teachers often use this type of score in assessments they develop, but test companies seldom, if ever, use them on norm-referenced tests.

Percentile Rank or Score A type of standard score reported on norm-referenced tests. This score indicates the percentage of people in the norm group who fell below the percentile rank of a particular test-taker. When discussing percentile scores, the appropriate phrasing is, "This student scored *at* the sixty-eighth percentile. That means he or she scored higher than 68 percent of the students in the norm group."

Raw Score Usually, this is the number of items a test-taker answers correctly on a norm-referenced test. It cannot be used to compare the student's performance on one subtest to her/his performance on another subtest.

Selected Response Test item that supplies an array of possible answers to a question. The student must choose the correct or best response from these possibilities. Examples include multiple-choice, true/false, and matching.

Standard Deviation A statistic that describes how much the scores in a distribution "spread out" around the mean. If you know the standard deviation, you know the "average" amount by which all of the test scores deviate from the mean score.

Standard Score Score that a raw score is converted to so that it can be used to compare a student's performance to the performance of students in the norm group. Standard scores convey how "high" or "low" a score is relative to the mean of the norm group.

Standardized Tests Tests constructed so that the questions, conditions for administration, scoring procedures, and score interpretations are "standardized" or consistent. There are two types of standardized tests: norm-referenced and criterion-referenced.

Stanine A standard score from 1 to 9. Stanines (short for "standard nine") are based on nine equal divisions of the normal curve, with each score representing a band on the curve rather than a point. Stanine scores of 4, 5, and 6 are considered "average."

Standard Error of Measurement (SEM) A type of standard deviation test companies use to calculate confidence intervals. If a person could take a test an infinite number of times with no learning between tests, the scores would, theoretically, form a normal distribution. Companies calculate an estimate of the standard deviation of these scores and use it to predict a range of scores within which the true score would fall. When the SEM is added and subtracted from an individual's *obtained score* to create a range of scores, the person's true score falls within this range (confidence interval) 68 percent of the time. For this reason, it is more realistic to assess a child's performance using the range of scores determined by the SEM than a single score.

True Score The average score that would result if a test-taker could take a test an infinite number of times with no learning occurring between tests. A true score exists only in theory. Because there is always error in the score, we can never know precisely what a student's true score is; we can say only that it falls within a certain range (confidence interval).

PART TWO

Making Tests Work for Children

CHAPTER FOUR

Creating Test-Friendly Environments

In the first section of this book, we explored reasons why the whole school community is responsible for helping children learn how to effectively demonstrate their knowledge on norm-referenced tests. If we were to synthesize those reasons into one sentence, it would be this: Tests matter in children's lives. A student's individual performance on norm-referenced tests may open or shut doors to opportunities, while students' collective performance, in districts that use test scores to guide resource allocation, may affect which opportunities are available. Responsibility for an academic experience that has such far-reaching impact must be shared if the school community believes in its children and wants them to succeed.

When the school community commits to helping children learn how to take tests, the community takes the first important step toward helping children master a literacy format that they will encounter repeatedly in both academic and work experiences. Such a commitment should address three essential areas: (1) ongoing, content-rich learning experiences, (2) effective whole-school test-taking environments, and (3) ethical test preparation interventions.

This chapter focuses principally on effective test-taking environments. In addition, we offer a brief caution about the relationship of learning experiences and norm-referenced test performance and lay the foundation for a workshop approach to ethical test preparation. The remainder of the book will emphasize the third area, ethical test preparation, by providing teacher-tested approaches that help make tests work for children. These approaches include classroom-based workshops for teachers whose children will be taking the tests (Chapters Five through Twelve). Chapter Thirteen suggests answers to common questions about the ethics of test preparation and offers many ways to integrate decision-making strategies used in test-taking situations into daily classroom life.

First, the caution. Workshops and strategies are no substitute for subject knowledge. They are *not* "quick fixes." If children do not know how to add, or read, or punctuate a sentence, test preparation workshops like ours will not help them learn these skills. If, however, children already have knowledge in the areas being assessed, the workshops will increase the likelihood that they will be able to demonstrate on the test what they know and can do.

Creating Effective Whole-School Test-Taking Environments

Let's consider some of the ways schools can help create good test-taking environments. There are many effective and common-sense approaches. Some, like removing distractions such as loud noise, are so obvious that it seems ludicrous to mention them, yet we cannot tell you how often we have encountered stories about mowing or leaf-blowing projects that coincided with test days. Others, like communicating with parents about the purpose and meaning of these tests, are perhaps equally obvious but more difficult to address.

Take a moment to jot down answers to the following three questions about how your own school creates effective test-taking environments.

1. What has your school community done to assure that the physical environment on the days of the test will be comfortable, quiet, and familiar?
2. What has your school community done to try to assure that the attitudes conveyed by teachers and parents support, rather than hinder, students' efforts?
3. What has your school community done to try to assure that the children will be nourished, rested, and emotionally prepared for the tests?

As we've talked with teachers and administrators at inservice sessions throughout the country, they have shared ideas and anecdotes. We have included some of their challenges and solutions as well as our own ideas to respond to these questions.

What has your school community done to assure that the physical environment on the days of the test will be comfortable, quiet, and familiar?

- Communication outside and within the school is essential. Consider what procedures your school has in place to coordinate testing days with buildings and grounds upkeep. Like us, you've probably heard or experienced horror stories about testing days being disturbed by jackhammers, mowers, leaf blowers, roof repair, etc. Similarly, communication within the school can assure that everyone is alert to the tests in progress. For instance, placing a moratorium on announcements over the PA, hanging signs outside doors that declare "testing in progress," or changing traffic patterns to decrease hallway noise are simple steps schools can take to create an appropriate testing environment.

- Think about whether children know the teachers or educational assistants who will administer the tests and whether they are in familiar settings. Many children find test-taking stressful. Familiar people and comfortable, customary settings relieve some of that stress. Although it may be efficient to use one proctor to test several classes at a time, it may not be productive. At one school we visited, the teachers lamented that for reasons of efficiency, the school had administered the test in one large room, with insufficient chairs to accommodate all of the children. These teachers felt that the testing conditions may have adversely affected the children's performance. Creative scheduling of educational assistants and classroom teachers may be necessary to best support children when they take norm-referenced tests.

- List the ways individual teachers in your school ensure that children are familiar with, and comfortable in, testing environments. Teachers use a variety of strategies to create these conditions, including playing appropriate music, adjusting room temperature, and role-playing testing situations and discussing children's reactions. Teachers should make every effort to "normalize" testing environments. One teacher, whose children normally worked in table groups, rehearsed the "working alone" setting of tests through "test drills" similar to fire drills. Periodically, she would signal the children to move their desks apart to complete a short activity by saying, "Go to your test places." By the time the test day arrived, the children were familiar with this testing position. Another teacher routinely asked children who worked in cooperative groups to set up and work in their private "offices." She wanted them to experience working on activities without help from their peers. These private "offices," created by cardboard dividers, became familiar signals for working without assistance. When test days arrived, the students were familiar with the work-alone condition.

What has your school community done to try to assure that the attitudes conveyed by teachers and parents support, rather than hinder, students' efforts?

- Think about how your school communicates to all parents and teachers about what the tests mean and how they should interpret the test scores. Many teachers and parents have little understanding of how test companies construct norm-referenced tests, what they intend the test to do, and what test scores mean. In addition, both teachers and parents bring attitudes toward tests that are often influenced by their past experiences with them. Inservice training is a worthwhile investment of time for teachers, while articles in school newsletters and discussions at parent meetings begin to get the word out to parents. District administrators who take the time to educate news reporters about the meaning and limits of score interpretation may find that their investment pays off when the article displaying local test scores appears in the paper.

■ Consider how your school helps teachers examine their own test-taking experiences and attitudes towards tests. Research indicates that teachers' attitudes can affect student performance. Unfortunately for children, research also indicates that teachers frequently have negative attitudes towards norm-referenced tests. Teachers communicate these attitudes to children in many ways. Casual hallway conversations with colleagues overheard by children, as well as other verbal and nonverbal messages, all convey to children whether or not teachers value the tests. As one teacher ruefully admitted, she knew that no matter what words she used, the kids could still see her "twitch" whenever she talked with them about tests. She had to resort to practicing in front of a mirror until she got so good in her presentation that "she almost believed herself."

What has your school community done to try to assure that the children will be nourished, rested, and emotionally prepared for the tests?

■ Outline the ways your school communicates with parents to let them know when the tests will take place and what they can do to physically and emotionally prepare their children. Teachers need to tell parents in a timely way that their children will be taking tests that are intellectually, physically, and emotionally demanding. Schools need to communicate in ways that reach all parents, including those who cannot read, who do not speak English, or who may not attend parent meetings because of work schedules or cultural barriers. For example, we know of schools that have located community members who translate letters home to parents, or visit homes to explain school matters in the parents' first language. However communication occurs, it should include reminders about the importance of plenty of rest and good nutrition. Schools also need to alert parents that some children may show signs of stress during testing and provide suggestions for ways to help their children relax.

■ Think about how your school and individual staff members attend to children's physical, emotional, and motivational needs during testing. There are many ways to create a positive environment for testing, though none substitutes for subject knowledge and an understanding of how to take tests. Some schools provide training for children and teachers on relaxation techniques and provide nutritious snacks before and during the tests. Individual teachers may use workshop procedures discussed later in this book to help children learn to express and manage their emotional reactions to the tests. Some schools hold spirit assemblies, while others work hard to create a "we can do it together" atmosphere through visual displays and verbal messages to the children. Others celebrate when the test is over. For example, one teacher built a sense of team spirit in the weeks before the test, reminding children that because they knew what to do, the test would be a "piece of cake." When the students completed the tests, several parents brought in cakes and the class celebrated their accomplishments.

This story raises an important issue about the judicious use of rewards and incentives to motivate children. In this case, the teacher used a particular phrase to reinforce children's confidence, and offered the cake as a surprise reward for the children's effort. However, we are also aware of another use of food that backfired. A teacher promised her students candy as soon as they "finished." You can imagine the results. Some schools offer very significant material rewards for high test performances, such as gift certificates, money, bicycles, etc. Whether it is candy or a bike, the consequences need to be carefully considered any time rewards are used as motivators.

Ethical Test Preparation: Laying the Foundation for a Workshop Approach

Ideally, your school will create an optimal test-taking environment. Even if it doesn't, teachers can help students learn to negotiate norm-referenced tests with more confidence and with a greater chance of accurately demonstrating their knowledge. The next several chapters describe in detail a process teachers can use, but the following two stories capture the essence of what this process is really about.

One of us, Sherry, has written a children's book, and librarians would occasionally invite her to read and speak about her book. What stands out for her about those readings was the question that children, even in upper elementary grades, asked her repeatedly: How did you find the time to write all those books? In fact, Sherry had created only one book. But to children who saw that multiple copies of the book existed and who interpreted what she said literally and within the framework of their limited writing experience, Sherry's announcement that she had written a book was bound to cause wonder. How, indeed, could she have found the time to write *all those books*?

You may be chuckling about the delightfully naive assumptions children bring to unfamiliar situations. But adults fall prey to their assumptions, as well. Consider this next story. Our friend, Gretchen, has beaten cancer, but when she first discovered the disease, she exacted a promise from her husband that he would learn to cook. She freely admits that she took advantage of him at a weak moment, but a deal's a deal. Although she has recovered superbly, Bob, at fifty-nine, is now responsible for preparing Sunday dinner. Like many of us who have tried to learn something new, he finds some difficult tasks unexpectedly easy, and a few simple tasks unexpectedly hard. Take onions, for example. A recipe said to chop the onion, but it did not say to peel it. Bob skillfully chopped. He neglected, however, to peel. Recounting this story, Gretchen wondered with good humor how anyone could eat for fifty-nine years and not know that onions first need to be peeled. She had simply assumed that he would know.

Both of these stories remind us that what baffles or confuses learners will remain a mystery unless we find ways to see the world through their eyes. We have designed these test preparation workshops to help teachers elicit from children the ways they make sense of the questions posed on multiple-choice, norm-referenced tests. When teachers listen to children explain their approaches to test items, they can use this assessment to help them understand the stumbling blocks those items pose, and adjust their instruction as needed. In this way, *assessment can begin to inform instruction,* the overarching principle that guides this work.

When we deliberately create opportunities to check our assumptions, we peel away the layers that may prevent us from seeing what makes a task confusing to kids. We increase the likelihood that we can anticipate and correct misunderstandings before they occur in a setting where the results matter. Even better, we decrease the odds that we'll be standing figuratively with Bob picking onion peels out of the dinner.

We have also designed these workshops to increase teachers' skills in helping children learn specific decision-making strategies. Five fundamental assumptions underlie the workshops.

1. Students can learn to negotiate the *literacy format* of a norm-referenced test.
2. Children learn about new literacy formats by constructing their understandings through active learning.
3. Test preparation interventions can be created that protect the integrity of children, curriculum, teachers, and the test.
4. Affective responses to test conditions influence performance.
5. Teachers have a responsibility to help children identify the coping skills and decision-making strategies that will help them negotiate standardized, multiple-choice tests and other unfamiliar situations.

The eight, carefully sequenced workshops built on these assumptions should take place over eight to ten days. Teachers should conduct the first seven workshops immediately prior to administration of the state assessment, and should administer the last workshop, a postassessment of the children's experiences, within a day or two after completion of the test. Each workshop lasts from thirty to sixty minutes. We provide an overview of the workshops in Figure 4.1.

Although we scripted the workshops to minimize teacher preparation, the scripts are only guides. We expect teachers to adapt the scripts as needed to make their delivery as natural as possible. Along these lines, teachers have told us that the workshops go more smoothly when they have practiced the scripts ahead of time, rather than reading them cold the day of the workshops.

We recommend that teachers follow the workshops in sequence, rather than choose a "little of this and a little of that." We believe that the time invested in the workshops is an important part of the curriculum—and not time taken *away* from it.

That said, we also expect that once teachers are familiar with the workshops, they will be able to integrate many of the strategies and concepts into children's learning throughout the year (see Chapter Thirteen). After teachers "normalize" these approaches by including them regularly in the curriculum, they may reduce the time spent in structured test preparation. What was once *new* will have become *review*.

Workshop Materials

The workshop materials include the overheads, preassessment and postassessment surveys, and practice tests referenced in the workshops (see Appendixes). The two practice tests contain items created to represent the variety of formats typical of norm-referenced tests. Items on the second practice test illustrate common stumbling blocks these types of tests present to children.

We recommend that teachers adapt the tests as needed to fit the format of those used in their state. For instance, if your state uses a multiple-choice test with four choices per item lettered alternately ABCD and EFGH, adjust the practice test materials to match the format of the bubble sheet your students will use on the real test. Because test formats differ, we have not included a bubble sheet. You will need to make copies of the bubble sheet from your particular state test for students to use during the workshops.

We designed the practice tests for students in third through fifth grades. If your students are in higher middle school grades, you may be able to use the sample practice tests your test company supplies (assuming your district has chosen to purchase them), and apply the workshop principles and strategies to them (see Figure 4.1). In this way, you can use items that more closely match the level of difficulty appropriate for your students.

Workshops at a Glance

The following table provides a quick reference to the purposes, procedures, and key principles for each of the workshops. Each student workshop is thoroughly explained in its own chapter.

The eight scripted, carefully-sequenced workshops take place over eight to ten days. The first seven should be conducted immediately prior to test administration. Each workshop lasts from thirty to sixty minutes.

DAY ONE: Preassessment

Task

1. Administer a survey to assess children's current attitudes toward, and previous experiences with, multiple-choice tests.

Purposes

1. Convey to children that the tests are important by asking them to think about their experiences and attitudes.
2. Provide a more realistic idea about children's actual attitudes (vs. teachers' assumptions).
3. Gather information that can help guide the workshops.
4. Collect baseline information that can be used to compare children's attitudes before and after the workshops and test have been completed.

Key Principles

1. Assumptions can get in the way of teaching and learning.
2. Assessment informs instruction.

FIGURE 4.1 Workshops at a Glance

DAYS TWO, THREE, and FOUR: Eliciting and Exploring Children's Reasoning and Emotional Responses

Tasks

1. Introduce children to test materials, marking procedures, and the importance of the test.
2. Administer the first practice test.
3. Use small-group and whole-group discussions to elicit ways children think about test items and respond emotionally.

Purposes

1. Let *children* teach each other by encouraging them through guided discussion to express their approaches to test items.
2. Legitimize children's feelings and provide strategies for dealing with them.
3. Compile a student-generated list of test-taking strategies.

Key Principles

1. Children can help each other learn.
2. Children have, or can develop, effective strategies for negotiating multiple-choice tests.
3. Emotions affect performance.

DAYS FIVE, SIX, and SEVEN: Teaching Children Strategies for Taking Tests

Tasks

1. Teach two strategies: *begin with what you know* and the *process of elimination.*
2. Practice these strategies through a second practice test.
3. Review each item to identify specific strategies children can use with particular types of items.

Purpose

1. Improve the likelihood children will be able to show what they know by increasing their skill in recognizing relevant clues, common distracters, and demands of various types of questions.

Key Principles

1. Effective decision-making strategies can be learned through modeling and practice.
2. Children can learn to identify relevant clues and distracters in multiple-choice tests.

> Administer tests. Record observations of children's behaviors and questions during the test. Use these observations in conjunction with the post-test survey to assess the effectiveness of the workshops and to suggest adaptations that may improve the workshops next time.

FIGURE 4.1 Workshops at a Glance, continued

DAY EIGHT: Postassessment

Tasks

1. Administer a survey to assess children's attitudes and feelings about the tests, the strategies they used, and perceptions of their performance.
2. Lead a group discussion about children's experiences with the tests, and have them generate advice they would give about the test to younger children.
3. Use the assessment to celebrate the class's achievement.

Purposes

1. Bring closure to the experience of taking the tests.
2. Collect data to help assess effectiveness of the workshops and to support any classroom-based research related to this topic.
3. Gather information that might lead to adaptations in the workshops or that might suggest ways to integrate workshop strategies into the curriculum.

Key Principles

1. Assessment and classroom-based research inform instruction.
2. Accomplishments deserve recognition.
3. Children can help each other learn.

FIGURE 4.1 Workshops at a Glance, continued

CHAPTER FIVE

Workshop One

Assessing Students' Expectations and Attitudes

Sometimes you have to learn things again and again. When we first started working with schools on norm-referenced tests, we heard many stories from teachers and children about how upsetting the tests were. We heard about children crying, pulling their hair, even fighting. So when we created the first posttest assessment, we included this item:

> Do you think practicing ahead of time helped you feel calmer and less worried about taking the test?
>
> A. Yes! I think practicing helped me feel less worried when I took the test.
>
> B. No! I don't think practicing made me feel any less worried.
>
> C. No! I think practicing made me feel *more* worried!

We thought we had covered all possible responses, until we read the response one student felt driven to write in. To our surprise and amused chagrin, our young informant noted tartly, "I wasn't worried to begin with!" We *know* that it's better to start with information about students than with assumptions—but we had to learn it once again.

Before beginning the test preparation workshops with your students, you will need to assess their expectations and attitudes towards multiple-choice tests. Use the written survey, "What Do You Think About Tests?" for this assessment (see Appendixes).

Taking time for this preassessment will signal to students that how they feel about these tests is important. It will also help them begin thinking about their knowledge of multiple-choice tests. By examining students' responses, you will learn what your students' preconceptions and prior experiences are. The survey will provide you with information about the range of your students' attitudes, feelings, and expectations about these tests. It will also begin the process of introducing test language that may be confusing.

During one of our teacher-training workshops, a teacher shared a story that was funny to the adults, but probably not as amusing to the child involved. She prefaced her story by commenting that she wished she had done this type of preassessment with her children. She had assumed when she told the children they would be taking the CAT test (*California Achievement Test*) that they would know what she meant. However, on the first day of the test she was amused and dismayed when one of her students arrived at school clutching her pet cat and explaining to the crossing guard that it was the day for the cat test. (We are not making this up! She swore this story was true.)

Administering the Preassessment Survey, "What Do You Think About Tests?"

1. Make a copy of the survey for each child in your class. If paper resources are limited, make an overhead transparency and have the children respond to the questions on their own paper.

2. Before administering the survey, tell the children that they will be taking a multiple-choice achievement test called _____ (name the test) in a few weeks. Tell them that today you would like to find out what kinds of experiences they have had with multiple-choice tests and how they feel about these types of tests. If the students say, "I've never taken an achievement test!", simply reassure them that you're interested in any experiences they've had with tests.

   Refrain from giving any explanation about the purpose or importance of the tests. You want to find out on this day what the *students* already have in mind. It's important to be neutral, and to avoid statements or attitudes that may bias the students' responses. You want to find out what the students are thinking or feeling, not what they think you want to hear.

   Do *not* tell the students, "Don't worry. These tests won't matter," or "Don't worry, the tests aren't important." These statements, however well-intended, send confusing messages to students. On the other hand, older students sometimes ask if the test scores will affect their grades. Teachers may worry that if they say no, the students will discount the importance of the test. Explaining that the scores do become part of the student's permanent record and that the overall academic record may affect educational and job opportunities may be helpful.

3. Read each item aloud to the students. Wait for the students to respond before proceeding to the next item.

4. Collect the surveys. Before the next day, tabulate the multiple-choice responses and read the answers to the open-ended questions. Use the information to inform the way you will guide your students through the workshops.
5. Save the surveys so that you can compare presurvey and postsurvey responses.

Afterthoughts

Originally the survey was much longer, but feedback from teachers helped us winnow some items down to those that currently appear. You, of course, should feel free to add items that are of interest to you.

Teachers have suggested that it might be useful to include this survey with a letter home to parents about the impending tests. They wondered if it might encourage parents to think about their own experiences with tests and their attitudes toward them. If you decide to try this, we would be very interested in hearing stories about parents' reactions to the surveys.

CHAPTER SIX

Workshop Two

Exploring Students' Reactions to Tests and Current Strategies

The best story we know about children and the magic of learning is the one we told in Chapter One about Taylor learning to ride a bike. We emphasized that all children deserve to experience similar moments of self-discovery, and to confirm that they have it within themselves to learn. Moreover, repeated moments of self-discovery are crucial, for every new learning situation presents its own challenges. Visit once again with Taylor, two years after the bicycle incident:

> Taylor's frustration with the challenges of long division was becoming increasingly apparent as she worked through problem after problem of her math homework. She mumbled to herself, erased vigorously, and squirmed in her seat. Finally, in exaspera- tion, she threw down her pencil and announced with all of the righteousness and certainty a nine-year-old could muster: "I already have all the math skills I'm ever going to need. I'm not going to be a cashier when I grow up."

The child who began riding her bike when she perceived she had the ability to learn that skill needed to discover that she could learn long division, as well. Yet, no learning about long division would take place until Taylor could manage her emotional response to the work. The first task, then, was to help her make decisions that would enable her to work through her feelings of incompetence and defeat. We can assist all children to meet the demands of new learning situations, including standardized tests, by arming them with effective decision- making strategies.

We will emphasize and review three fundamental decision- making strategies over the course of these workshops:

1. Identifying emotional reactions to unfamiliar situations and finding ways to manage those reactions effectively.
2. Developing skills in understanding what new situations require.

3. Learning to select a decision-making strategy that will be useful in a particular situation.

The core of today's work is to have children take a multiple-choice test under timed conditions. (If your state test is not timed, don't worry about the timed component of this workshop.) This testing situation may be new and uncomfortable for many of them. You may be uncomfortable, as well. You may feel that the practice test questions are too hard and may instinctively want to make things easier for your students. However, we have designed the experience to elicit a wide range of emotional reactions, and to bring to the surface children's current strategies. Rather than change the items, take this opportunity to explore with your students how they were feeling, and what they did to make sense of the test questions.

These are the five steps that you will complete with your students on this second day.

1. Set the tone for the workshop and establish its purpose.
2. Introduce the materials and bubble sheet marking procedure.
3. Complete a practice test.
4. Discuss students' reactions, feelings, and strategies.
5. Build the bridge to the next day's workshop.

Step 1: Set the Tone for the Workshop and Establish Its Purpose.

Script

"In a few weeks you will be taking a test called _____. How many of you have taken tests that used booklets that looked like these or that used this type of answer sheet?" *SHOW BOOKLET AND BUBBLE SHEET.*

"These kinds of tests can be a challenge so we're going to spend some time figuring out the best ways to go about taking them. We're going to practice some questions today in reading and math and then we're going to talk about them." *EMPHASIZE THAT THIS IS PRACTICE AND THAT YOU KNOW YOU'RE OUT OF YOUR ROUTINE BUT THAT YOU THINK THIS IS IMPORTANT.*

"I think it's *really* important for you to learn how to take tests like these because they'll keep popping up during middle school and high school. I think you'll feel a lot happier and more confident if you can learn this year how to make these tests work for you. Some of you may not be thinking about what you're going to do after high school just yet, but you need to know that some people go on to more schooling. Most schools that people go to in order to learn a job or a craft or a trade use tests similar to these to decide who gets in. Does anybody know someone who had to take a test to get a job or to get into a school?" *ALLOW CHILDREN TO REPLY.*

"Learning to take a test well is kind of like learning to play soccer or an instrument, or learning to use a computer. It takes practice, but you feel good when you know what to do."

Step 2: Introduce the Materials and Bubble Sheet Marking Procedure.

For this demonstration, you need to have practice test booklets, bubble sheets, guide strips, the sample question below written on the board, and a diagram on the board of two lines of a bubble sheet. Guide strips can be three-by-five-inch index cards or strips of tag board.

Write this sample question on the board:

The kids can see the bird in the tall _____.
A. tree
B. ball
C. get
D. mat

Draw a sample bubble sheet on the board like the one below.

1. ○   ○   ○   ○
  A   B   C   D
2. ○   ○   ○   ○
  A   B   C   D

Script

"In case you haven't taken a test like this or in case you've forgotten, first you need to read the question, and when you're ready to give an answer, you completely fill in the correct bubble or circle." DO THE PROBLEM THAT'S ON THE BOARD TOGETHER.

"Do you know why it's so important to fill in only one bubble?" IF NO STUDENT CAN PROVIDE THE CORRECT ANSWER, TELL THEM.

"Your answer sheets on the real test are graded by a computer that senses the marks of the pencil. If you have more than one bubble filled in, if you don't erase well, or if you don't fill the bubble completely, *the computer just won't get it.*" IF YOU THINK IT'S APPROPRIATE, MAKE A BIG DEAL ABOUT THE COMPUTER NOT BEING SMART ENOUGH TO FIGURE OUT WHAT YOU MEANT.

"So, make sure you fill in the bubble completely, that your marks are pretty dark, and that you don't go outside the lines of the circle. Fill in *one* bubble on each line. If you want to change your answer, erase completely.

"Oh, the other thing the computer has trouble with—it can't tell if you've gotten off track. You must make sure that for Question 1 in the question booklet, you fill in the bubble next to the number 1 on the answer sheet. To help you with this, we will use these guides during the practice test and during the real test." ON THE BOARD, SHOW THE STUDENTS HOW TO LINE UP THE GUIDE UNDER THE NUMBER AND BUBBLES, HOW TO CHECK THAT THE NUMBER ON THE SHEET IS THE SAME ONE AS THE NUMBER NEXT TO THE QUESTION, AND HOW TO MOVE THE GUIDE IN THE APPROPRIATE DIRECTION ON THE ANSWER SHEET.

Step 3: Complete a Practice Test.

List these reminders on a chart that will be visible to the students during the test:

1. Use your guide to make sure that the number next to the question and the number on your answer sheet are the same.
2. Mark only one bubble on a line.
3. Work by yourself.
4. Keep working until time is called. Answer as many questions as you can.

Script

"I'm going to give you the practice test now. There's a booklet with directions and questions and a separate sheet where you mark your answers. You need to remember that when you take these tests, you can't work together like you sometimes do. You have to stay in your seats, be quiet, and keep working until time is up. I know it's hard to do all those things and *that's why we're practicing*. You will have fifteen minutes to work on the test. You may not get finished—that often happens on these types of tests. Just keep working until I tell you time is up. While you work, I will be walking around the room. I won't be able to help you answer the questions; do your best, on your own."

(NOTE: DEPENDING ON THE AGE AND/OR GENERAL ABILITY OF YOUR STUDENTS, YOU MAY NEED TO SHORTEN OR LENGTHEN THE TIME ALLOWED. HOWEVER, YOU NEED TO KEEP THE TEST TIME SHORT ENOUGH TO CREATE SOME ANXIETY SO THE ACTUAL TEST CONDITIONS ARE SIMULATED. IF YOUR STATE TESTS ARE NOT TIMED, APPROXIMATE THE CONDITIONS UNDER WHICH YOUR STUDENTS WILL BE WORKING.)

STUDENTS WORK ON THE TEST. PLEASE DO NOT HELP THEM. INSTEAD, OBSERVE TO SEE WHO IS AND IS NOT FOLLOWING THE GUIDELINES YOU SET UP. WATCH FOR SIGNS OF DISTRESS AND MAKE A POINT OF TALKING WITH THOSE CHILDREN LATER TO FIND OUT WHAT'S GOING ON.

TAKE A STRETCH BREAK AFTER THE TEST AND THEN DEBRIEF USING THE FOLLOWING PROCEDURE.

> **We think that the debriefings or reflections after each practice session are the key to helping the children understand how to be successful on these types of tests.**

Step 4: Discuss Students' Reactions, Feelings, and Strategies.

Script

"Okay, you did it! Great. I noticed _____." *GIVE WHATEVER POSITIVE FEEDBACK IS APPROPRIATE, AND REINFORCE EXAMPLES RELATED TO THE GUIDELINES.*

ON THE BOARD, LABEL TWO COLUMNS "BEFORE" AND "AFTER." GIVE THE FOLLOWING DIRECTIONS TO THE STUDENTS.

"Please get out a piece of paper. Write down or draw ways you were feeling *before* you took this practice test and ways you're feeling *now*. Go ahead. Work alone." *GIVE THEM FOUR OR FIVE MINUTES TO RECORD THEIR FEELINGS.*

"Let's hear how some of you were feeling. Tell me about some of your 'Before' feelings or show me your pictures and describe them."

LIST THE FEELINGS AND VALIDATE EACH CHILD'S CONTRIBUTION. POINT TO SIMILARITIES AND DIFFERENCES. THEN DO THE "AFTER" COLUMN. WHEN YOU COMPLETE THE "AFTER" COLUMN, SUMMARIZE THE CHILDREN'S CONVERSATION BY SAYING:

"People have lots of different feelings about tests like these. Some people feel _____. Other people feel _____."

USE THE LANGUAGE YOUR STUDENTS HAVE PROVIDED. HOWEVER, IF YOUR STUDENTS' RESPONSES DO NOT COVER THE FULL RANGE OF REACTIONS (ANXIOUS/WORRIED TO EXCITED/CHALLENGED), BE SURE TO INCLUDE THE REACTIONS NOT REPORTED.

"Sometimes people feel worried because they get confused or because they can't figure out what the test wants them to do. Sometimes people say they are bored or scared because they've never taken a test like this and they're just not used to it.

"I want all of you to feel confident and at ease because then your brains can do their best work. Here's the thing that's really neat: These tests are kind of like puzzles or sports or games. You can figure out what you're supposed to do by practicing and talking to other people, and then you can feel good about the challenge of doing your best.

"Let's talk for five minutes about different ways you went about taking this test. Tell me some things you did to figure out what to do on this test."

THIS IS JUST A GENERAL OPENING FOR KIDS TO HEAR THAT PEOPLE GO ABOUT TEST-TAKING IN DIFFERENT WAYS. ACKNOWLEDGE AND SUPPORT THEIR RESPONSES. WATCH FOR COMMENTS LIKE "I READ THROUGH AND DO ALL THE ONES I KNOW FIRST," "I READ THE ANSWERS BEFORE I READ THE PASSAGE," AND "I ELIMINATE ANSWERS I KNOW CAN'T BE RIGHT." START A CHART THAT YOU WILL ADD TO FOR THE NEXT SEVERAL DAYS CALLED "GOOD IDEAS FOR TAKING TESTS," "TEST-TAKING STRATEGIES," "TRY THESE," OR WHATEVER SEEMS APPROPRIATE FOR YOUR CLASSROOM.

Step 5: Build a Bridge to the Next Day's Workshop.

Script

"Tomorrow I'll bring these tests back to you. I'll tell you the answers given by the test-maker and we'll work on figuring out ways to take the test so that you can answer as many questions as possible the way the test-maker would answer them."

Teachers' Homework

For Questions 8, 10, 12 , and 13, tally the number of responses for each possible answer. However, don't mark the students' answers right or wrong on their answer sheets. Keep your tallies on a separate piece of paper.

For example, on Question 8, your tally sheet could look like this:

A. 4 (kids marked this as correct)
B. 6 (kids marked this as correct)
C. 10 (kids marked this as correct)
D. 4 (kids marked this as correct)
Correct answer: B

Using the copies provided for Questions 8, 10, 12, and 13, make overhead transparencies and enter your tallies. Take the overheads, tally sheet, test booklets, and the children's answer sheets to school for the next day's workshop.

(Note: In the unlikely event only one child in the class selects an option, we strongly recommend you either "fudge" in your presentation of the results to the class, or select a question where at least two children selected each response, and create a new overhead. You want to convey to children that they are not alone in their choices, even though their reasons for those choices may vary.)

For assessment purposes, you may want to make tallies for as many questions as possible so that you will have a better understanding of how your children are reasoning and problem solving. We realize, however, that your time is limited and this may not be possible. Regardless of the number of questions you tally, be alert for items where a substantial number of children have marked the same wrong answer. You can use these as teaching points during the daily practice sessions.

CHAPTER SEVEN

Workshop Three
Thinking Allowed; Thinking Aloud

One afternoon a group of fourth-graders was talking about an item on a practice test. In order to answer the question accurately, the children needed to recognize that the word "train" has more than one meaning. One child plaintively queried, "How did you know the answer was train?" Another child responded, "Look at this sentence. It says there were four boxcars on the *blank*."

"So?" replied the first child.

"Well, I've read 'Boxcar Children' books and when I read the sentence on the test, I thought of the book and then I thought of trains."

"Oh!" exclaimed the first child. "I didn't know you could think of things outside the test to figure out the answers."

One of the most aggravating things about norm-referenced tests is that the test-taker never finds out which of her answers were correct or incorrect. There is no provision to help learning occur—no possibilities for modifying ineffective behaviors or expanding knowledge of test-taking strategies. We believe that children get better at selecting good answers by listening to and discussing the reasons people choose particular responses. The story above is an example of how this process works. Students also become more proficient at selecting "correct" responses when they participate in guided discussions exploring why a response *is* correct. Today's workshop allows students to experience both of these processes. They will have an opportunity to explain their own reasoning and listen to that of others. In addition, they will have the opportunity to work collaboratively to figure out why an answer is the correct one.

This workshop will be most effective if students have ample opportunity to discuss their reasoning. It should not be conducted as a drill-and-practice session where students merely call out the correct response.

These are the three steps that you will complete with your students on this third day.

1. Elicit students' reasoning in a large-group discussion.
2. Discuss test answers in small groups.
3. Help the whole group generate a list of useful test-taking strategies.

Step 1: Elicit Students' Reasoning in a Large-Group Discussion.

Script

"Here's what I did with the practice tests you took yesterday." *SHOW OVERHEAD QUESTION 8, BUT COVER THE LINE AT THE BOTTOM THAT GIVES THE CORRECT ANSWER.*

"For each question, I went through and counted how many people picked each answer. Would someone read this first question to us?" *CHOOSE A STUDENT TO READ THE QUESTION.*

"You can see here on the transparency that _____ people selected answer 'A,' _____ selected answer 'B,' _____ selected answer 'C,' and _____ people selected answer 'D.' It doesn't matter right now which answer *you* chose. I want you to see if you can explain why someone might have selected answer 'A.'" *TAKE SUGGESTIONS. MOVE STEADILY THROUGH EACH ANSWER. THIS IS NOT THE PLACE FOR YOU TO EXPLAIN WHY RESPONSES ARE INCORRECT. THE PURPOSE OF THIS EXERCISE IS TO ENCOURAGE THE STUDENTS TO SHARE THEIR REASONING AND TO LEARN FROM THE REASONING OF THEIR PEERS.*

"People had different reasons for the answers they gave. Some made sense, some may have been guesses. This is the answer the test-maker wanted you to give." *SHOW THEM THE CORRECT ANSWER.*

"Let's talk about why this is the 'right' answer. Who has some ideas?" *WATCH TO SEE HOW THE CHILDREN DEALT WITH THE DIRECTIONS. WHAT CLUES WERE THEY USING TO FIGURE OUT THE ANSWER? REINFORCE AND EMPHASIZE REASONING THAT LED TO THE CORRECT ANSWER.*

GO THROUGH THE SAME PROCEDURE WITH QUESTIONS 10, 12, AND 13, BEING SURE TO POINT OUT, IF NONE OF THE CHILDREN MENTION IT, THAT QUESTION 10 IS ABOUT FOLLOWING DIRECTIONS. FOR QUESTION 12, MAKE SURE THE CHILDREN REALIZE THEY CAN REWRITE THE PROBLEM ON SCRATCH PAPER IN VERTICAL FORM. LISTEN CAREFULLY FOR CHILDREN'S RECOGNITION THAT QUESTION 13 IS ASKING FOR A NUMBER SENTENCE, NOT A CALCULATION.

Step 2: Discuss Test Answers in Small Groups.

You should form discussion groups that have a good chance of working effectively together. However, if you do not typically ask children to work in cooperative groups, now is probably not the best time to begin. You may want to continue in the large-group format, making sure that students offer their ideas, rather than wait to hear the answers from you. In either case, give the students the test booklets and their original answer sheets. If you use small groups, you will alternate between giving directions and information and listening as students talk in small groups and report back to the whole group. If you use the whole-group format, you will give directions and information and facilitate the students' discussion. The directions that follow are for the small-group format. Adapt them as necessary for a whole-group approach.

Script

"Everyone find the first reading selection in the test on page 1. It's a paragraph with four blanks in it. Each blank is numbered beginning with 1. Read the question and the possible answers for blank 1." WAIT WHILE STUDENTS READ.

"The test-maker says that 'B' is the correct answer. There are two things I want you to do in your group:

1. Talk together and figure out *why* the answer is supposed to be 'B.'
2. Talk about how you could figure that out.

"In a few minutes I'll ask one person in each group to tell me what your group figured out." ON THIS FIRST ATTEMPT, GIVE THEM JUST THREE OR FOUR MINUTES FOR DISCUSSION.

CALL ON A STUDENT.

"Tell me what your group decided. Why is this the correct answer? What strategies could you use to figure that out?" GET AS MANY GROUPS TO RESPOND AS SEEMS USEFUL OR REASONABLE BUT CALL ON AT LEAST TWO. THEN ASK IF ANY OTHER GROUPS CAME UP WITH REASONS THAT HAVEN'T BEEN SHARED. HERE ARE SOME RESPONSES YOU SHOULD LISTEN FOR: STUDENTS LOOKED FOR CLUES IN THE DIRECTIONS; STUDENTS IDENTIFIED INFORMATION IN THE QUESTION THAT HELPED; STUDENTS IDENTIFIED AND ELIMINATED ANSWERS THAT WERE CLEARLY INCORRECT; STUDENTS MADE CONNECTIONS TO PRIOR KNOWLEDGE OR BACKGROUND INFORMATION THAT WAS HELPFUL.

GO THROUGH THE SMALL-GROUP/WHOLE-GROUP PROCEDURE TO FINISH UP THAT FIRST READING SELECTION (QUESTIONS 2, 3, AND 4).

AS THE STUDENTS SHARE HOW THEY COULD FIGURE OUT THE CORRECT RESPONSES FOR THE BLANKS IN THE PASSAGE, REINFORCE STRATEGIES THAT INVOLVE READING AHEAD AND MAKING SURE THAT EACH SENTENCE MAKES SENSE IN RELATION TO THE OTHER SENTENCES. ALSO REINFORCE THE STRATEGY OF READING THE WHOLE PASSAGE BEFORE BEGINNING TO SELECT ANSWERS.

Step 3: Help the Whole Group Generate a List of Useful Test-Taking Strategies.

Script

CLOSE THE SESSION BY COLLECTING THE BOOKLETS AND ANSWER SHEETS AND SAYING: "You've done a great job today working on these test questions [*OR AS CLOSE TO THAT AS IS TRUTHFUL!*]. Let's end this session by adding some ideas to our chart. What are some things you learned today about figuring out how to answer questions on this type of test?"

Remember to chart strategies.

Afterthoughts

One of the most challenging aspects of leading a discussion is to resist providing the answers, especially if the children are slow in sharing their ideas. As you probably know, children are very smart about getting adults to tell or show them things they could have figured out on their own. There are two strategies you may find useful. First, wait. Wait longer. Count silently to ten. Rephrase your question and wait again. Second, turn children's questions directed to you back to the group. For example, if a child asks you why "C" was the correct answer, ask the group for their ideas.

CHAPTER EIGHT

Workshop Four

Figuring Out What Works and Why

The teacher read aloud the item, "Which of these does not belong in this group? April, June, September, or December?"

"December!" the child responded quickly.

"That's correct. Tell me how you decided the answer was December," the teacher requested. She waited for the child to explain that December was the only month that had more than thirty days.

Instead, the child replied, "Because Christmas is in December, and it's not in any of those other months."

The primary purpose of these workshops is to help children use effective problem-solving strategies under norm-referenced testing conditions. However, as the story above indicates, children can get correct answers using creative reasoning that adults may not anticipate. Therefore, the workshops are valuable to teachers as well. Listening to children talk about how they think can help teachers understand what children know and how they make sense of their world. This form of assessment informs instruction.

You'll need to take about thirty minutes today to continue discussing items from the first practice test. The questions we chose for review help point out useful strategies or common pitfalls the students need to be aware of. After the discussion, ask the children what they've learned and add their ideas to your chart of test strategies. Keep reminding your students about the mindlessness of computers, the need to mark one bubble darkly, and how the guide strips can help them stay in the right place on the answer sheet.

These are the two steps that you will complete with your students on this fourth day.

1. Discuss test answers in small groups and report back to the whole group.
2. Help the whole group generate a list of useful test-taking strategies.

Step 1: Discuss Test Answers in Small Groups and Report Back to the Whole Group.

You should form discussion groups that have a good chance of working effectively together. Give the students test booklets and their original answer sheets. You will be working back and forth between giving directions and information and listening as students talk together in small groups and report back to the whole group.

Script

"Everyone find Question 7 in the test booklet. Read the question and the possible answers." *Wait while students read.*

"The test-maker says that 'C' is the correct answer. Just like yesterday, I want you to do two things in your group:

1. Talk together and figure out *why* the answer is supposed to be 'C.'
2. Talk about how you could figure that out.

"In a few minutes I'll ask one person in each group to tell me what your group figured out." *Give them just four or five minutes for discussion.*

Call on a student.

"Tell me what your group decided. Why is this the correct answer? What strategies could you use to figure that out?" *Get as many groups to respond as seems useful or reasonable but call on at least two. Then ask if any other groups came up with reasons that haven't been shared. Here are some responses you should listen for: students looked for clues in the directions; student identified information in the question that helped; students identified and eliminated answers that were clearly incorrect; students made connections to prior knowledge or background information that was helpful.*

Help children realize that they don't need to panic and abandon the game if they don't know the meaning of all the words. In Question 7, children may not recognize "Latin" or the term, "modern words." Yet, they can examine the last part of the directions and the answers and figure out what they're supposed to do.

Use the small-group/whole-group procedure to examine Questions 9, 11, 19, and 21.

Please note: Use Questions 9 and 11 to reinforce the importance of reading the directions very carefully. Use Question 21 to illustrate the importance of reading and understanding the question before reading the passage.

At this point the children will have explored thirteen of the twenty-two test questions. If you think it would be useful, use the same format to review the remaining nine questions (Questions 5,

6, 14, 15, 16, 17, 18, 20, AND 22). OR, FOR EACH QUESTION, SIMPLY TELL THE CHILDREN THE CORRECT RESPONSE AND ASK ONE STUDENT HOW HE OR SHE WOULD FIGURE IT OUT.

Step 2: Help the Whole Group Generate a List of Useful Test-Taking Strategies.

Script

"You've done a great job today working on these test questions [*OR AS CLOSE TO THAT AS IS TRUTHFUL!*]. Let's end this session by adding some more ideas to our chart. What are some things you learned today about figuring out how to answer questions on this type of test?"

Remember to chart strategies.

Afterthoughts

You can leave the chart of strategies visible in the room when the children actually take the state test. Teachers have told us that having the chart in place helped them out of the bind they felt when children would ask for help that teachers could not ethically provide in order to maintain the integrity of the test. With the chart in the room, they could say, "Look at our chart. What strategy might help you figure out a way to answer that question?"

CHAPTER NINE

Workshop Five

Thinking Inside and Outside the Box

Lee came home one afternoon fuming about a particular test item. "Mom," he said, "I was supposed to figure out which word would fit in two different sentences. One sentence said something about 'closing the kitchen *blank.*' The other sentence was about the '*blank* that advises the president.' I read all four choices and *none* of them would go with both sentences. I'm really mad because I spent so much time trying to figure out the answer that I couldn't finish the test."

Children are sometimes "boxed in" by preconceived ideas they bring to new problem-solving situations. In this story, Lee was boxed in by his conviction that he needed to struggle with a test item until he figured it out. However, because he did not know the technical term that describes people who advise the president, he could not answer the question. If he could have called on a repertoire of problem-solving strategies, he might have been able to break the impasse, reduce his frustration, and answer additional items.

Lee's preconception is only one of many. For instance, some children may equate guessing with cheating. ("But if the test-maker wants to find out what I know, and I don't really know it, isn't it cheating to guess? What if I guess right? That won't really tell the test-maker what I know.") Other children become anxious under timed conditions when they hear the sound of their classmates turning pages. They believe the other children must be smarter and quicker.

The first four days of workshops have focused on helping children identify effective test-taking strategies they currently use. *This workshop begins the process of introducing and naming specific strategies for them to practice.* Being aware of these strategies is important because of children's preconceptions and because test-makers design some items on norm-referenced tests with the expectation that many children will find them difficult. However, even when children don't know an answer, there are ways to narrow down the choices and move more efficiently through the test.

These are the four steps that you will complete with your students on this fifth day.

1. Review problem-solving strategies identified already.
2. Introduce two problem-solving strategies: (a) begin with what you know, and (b) use the process of elimination.
3. Administer Practice Test 2.
4. Elicit students' reactions to the test.

Step 1: Review Problem-Solving Strategies Identified Already.

Script

"Today, we're going to take another timed practice test. You will have twenty minutes to complete the test. Let's take a few minutes (without looking at the chart!) to review the test-taking strategies we already know. Who wants to name one?" *QUICKLY REVIEW STRATEGIES*.

"In addition to some of the strategies you already know, some of the most important decision-making strategies you can *learn* are what to do when you have to do something in a limited amount of time, when you don't know an answer, or when you're not sure what to do. I want to talk about two strategies that might help in these kinds of situations. I'm going to start with an example of a situation outside the classroom."

Step 2: Introduce Two Problem-Solving Strategies: (a) Begin with What You Know, and (b) Use the Process of Elimination.

Script

"Imagine you are at a soccer camp. The coach announces he will give an award to players who earn fifteen points in five minutes. You can earn five points by dribbling the ball down the field, five points each time you kick the ball into the goal, five points by passing the ball to another player, and five points for dribbling the ball through an obstacle course. You are really good at kicking goals and passing. Which activities will you do in order to quickly earn enough points for an award?" *ELICIT RESPONSES, LOOKING FOR SOMEONE TO SAY THAT THEY WOULD KICK GOALS OR PASS THE BALL TO ANOTHER PLAYER. THEN ASK THEM WHY THEY WOULD DO THAT. YOU WANT TO REINFORCE THE REASONING STRATEGY THAT UNDER TIMED CONDITIONS, YOU SHOULD BEGIN WITH WHAT YOU KNOW. EVEN IF YOUR STATE TEST IS NOT TIMED, BEGINNING WITH WHAT YOU KNOW CAN HELP BUILD CHILDREN'S CONFIDENCE.*

REMEMBER, IF YOUR STATE TEST IS UNTIMED, YOU WILL NEED TO ADAPT THIS STORY TO REFLECT THE REQUIREMENTS OF THE TEST.

"You have just used a problem-solving strategy called 'begin with what you know.' You can also use that strategy when you take tests, and it is one of two problem-solving strategies we're going to practice today.

"See if you can figure out what the other strategy is by the example I'm going to give you now.

"If you wanted to buy a bicycle, you might go to the store with your parents and look at all the bicycles the store had. What kind of features might you look for on a bicycle?" *ELICIT A FEW RESPONSES.*

"Let's say you found four bicycles you really liked that had the features you wanted. But your parents can't spend too much money so they tell you that you can buy a bicycle if it costs less than $150. The four bicycles you've chosen cost $110, $140, $175, and $200. What would you have to do? Let's assume that you have no other resources for money so you really can't spend more than $150." *ELICIT RESPONSES, LOOKING FOR SOMEONE TO SAY THEY WOULD ELIMINATE THE TWO MORE EXPENSIVE BIKES FROM CONSIDERATION.*

"You have just used a problem-solving strategy called the 'process of elimination.' You can also use that strategy when you take tests, and it's the second strategy we're going to practice today."

Step 3: Administer Practice Test 2.

Script

"We're going to take the practice test today a little differently than we took the first test. Get out your guide strips, a pencil, and a piece of paper. I'm going to pass out the tests and the bubble sheet you used before. Please do not begin reading until I tell you to." *PASS OUT TESTS, BUBBLE SHEETS, AND GUIDE STRIPS TO THOSE CHILDREN WHO MAY HAVE LOST THEM. MAKE SURE THAT CHILDREN HAVE A SCRATCH PIECE OF PAPER.*

"Let's all look at page 1 together. There are three items. We have a problem with rectangles, a box with missing numbers, and a subtraction problem. Remember our story about the soccer camp and how you should begin with what you know?

"In a moment, I'm going to ask you to look over the questions on this page. I'm *not* asking you to read every question thoroughly, and I'm *not* asking you to answer every question right now. I want you to read the question just enough to decide if you think you can answer it fairly easily and only answer it if you think you can.

"The question you choose may not be Question 23, and that's fine. Here's why.

"These tests contain questions with information that you already know or can figure out, and they also contain questions that have information you don't know. Since you have only a limited amount of time to take this test, it's better to put your effort into answering the questions you can fairly easily figure out. Don't worry, we'll come back to the questions you skip over now.

"So, let's begin. Look over the questions on page 1 and find a question you feel pretty sure you can answer.

"When you find a question you can answer, check to see what number it is. Then, make sure your guide strip is under the same number on the answer sheet. Answer that question by filling in the correct bubble on your answer sheet."

WAIT UNTIL YOU SEE THAT THE MAJORITY OF THE STUDENTS HAVE COMPLETED ONE QUESTION.

"It looks like everyone has answered one question. Let's keep going. Look for the next question you can answer. That question may be on page 1 or it may be on one of the next pages. When you find the question, remember to make sure that the guide strip is under the same number on the answer sheet as the question you are answering. What's the name of this strategy that we're using? 'Begin with what you know!'

"Go ahead and answer the question."

CONTINUE THIS DIRECTED PROCESS AS LONG AS YOU THINK IT IS NECESSARY. WHEN THE STUDENTS SEEM TO UNDERSTAND, DIRECT THEM TO CONTINUE UNTIL THEY REACH THE END OF THE TEST.

(NOTE: THE STRATEGY OF DOING WHAT YOU KNOW FIRST IS ONE OF THE MOST DIFFICULT FOR CHILDREN TO FOLLOW, BUT IT IS VERY IMPORTANT. DON'T TURN THE STUDENTS LOOSE ON THIS ONE TOO QUICKLY.)

WHEN THE STUDENTS HAVE FINISHED GOING THROUGH THE TEST AND DOING WHAT THEY KNOW, YOU WILL GIVE THEM INSTRUCTIONS ABOUT USING THE PROCESS OF ELIMINATION STRATEGY. THEY WILL THEN GO BACK THROUGH THE TEST TO PRACTICE THE PROCESS OF ELIMINATION STRATEGY ON THE ITEMS THEY SKIPPED.

"Now that you have finished answering the questions you know, you will need to go back and try to answer the questions you skipped. You are going to practice your second major strategy: 'the process of elimination.' You can use this strategy on items you feel pretty sure about, but it may be especially helpful with items you're not as sure of. On any test, you need to go back and try to answer questions you skipped, as long as there is time.

"Let's practice how you might use the process of elimination."

PUT THIS SIMPLE ADDITION PROBLEM ON THE BOARD.

66 + 23 =

A. 12 R1
B. 99
C. 87
D. 89

"Who can tell me how the process of elimination strategy might work with this item? What answers could you quickly eliminate and why?" *YOU WANT TO HEAR CHILDREN ELIMINATE "A" BECAUSE R1 SIGNALS A DIVISION PROBLEM, AND THIS IS AN ADDITION PROBLEM. YOU ALSO WANT TO HEAR THEM ELIMINATE "C" BECAUSE IF YOU ADD THE ONES COLUMN, YOU KNOW THE ANSWER MUST END IN 9.*

"We're going to finish the test now. Remember to use your guide strips. You will have ten minutes to finish the test." *AFTER TEN MINUTES, TELL THE STUDENTS TIME IS UP AND COLLECT ALL THE MATERIALS.*

Step 4: Elicit Students' Reactions to the Test.

Give the children a chance to share their immediate reactions to the test. You might try a quick "thumbs up/thumbs down." Tell them you want them to call out one word that describes how they feel about today's test. Go around the room in sequence, with each person signaling with their thumbs and saying their word. It's fun, physical, and gives you a quick assessment of their gut reactions.

Script

"When you were taking the test, did you notice when people were turning pages of the test? How did that make you feel?" *ELICIT THEIR REACTIONS. SOME KIDS MAY SAY IT MADE THEM ANXIOUS THAT SOME PEOPLE WERE MOVING FASTER THROUGH THE TEST THAN THEY WERE.*

"Remember that when you hear the sounds of pages turning, that may mean people are going through the test to find questions they know they can answer. It doesn't necessarily mean that people are finishing quicker than you are. They may just be practicing a good decision-making strategy. Tomorrow we'll go over the answers of the test and talk more about decision-making strategies."

CHAPTER TEN

Workshop Six

Solving the Mystery of Multiple-Choice Tests

One day Kathryn overheard us talking with another young woman about a decision-making strategy related to reading comprehension subtests. As we were explaining the importance of reading the questions before reading the passages, a bewildered expression crossed Kathryn's face. She interrupted, exclaiming, "I always thought it was cheating to look back at the passages once you started reading the questions!" When questioned, she revealed that she always approached multiple-choice comprehension tests by reading a passage all the way through and then diligently avoiding even glancing at the material as she tried to answer the questions. Needless to say, this strategy hampered her ability to demonstrate her comprehension.

This story is another example of how children are sometimes boxed in by their preconceived ideas. At other times, children think so far outside the box that they resist attempts to limit their thinking. For example, we've heard many times about children who reason their way to a "wrong" answer based on personal values or creative logic. Sometimes children don't even *see* the box. One of our daughters took a sample test and missed every item where the question was phrased in the negative, i.e., "Which of these is *not* . . . ?" When her teacher pointed out the format and pattern of her responses, she was able to easily correct her mistakes. In this case, the test had not measured what she knew, but rather tested her familiarity with a particular format. Today's workshop will continue to broaden the range of strategies children might use to solve problems.

In this workshop, you will systematically work through half the items on the second practice test with your students. The format will be teacher-guided whole-group discussion.

These are the two steps for today's workshop.

1. Assess students' use of the strategy "begin with what you know."
2. Review the first seven items of Practice Test 2.

Step 1: Assess Students' Use of the Strategy "Begin with What You Know."

Pass out the students' test booklets and answer sheets.

Script

"One of the strategies we talked about last time was the strategy 'begin with what you know.' Think about the way you took this practice test. If you went through the test and answered questions you were pretty sure of first, show me 'thumbs up.' If you didn't, show me 'thumbs down.'"

THIS IS A QUICK ASSESSMENT FOR YOU, THE TEACHER, AND IT ALSO REINFORCES THE STRATEGY. ELICIT FROM THE STUDENTS THEIR IDEAS ABOUT THE WAYS THIS PROCESS MAY HAVE HELPED AS WELL AS THE WAYS IT MAY HAVE PRESENTED DIFFICULTIES. DEVELOP THIS CONVERSATION AS YOU THINK APPROPRIATE.

Step 2: Review the First Seven Items of Practice Test 2.

Write these questions on the board:

1. How did you feel when you read this question?
2. What did the question ask you to do?
3. Could you use the process of elimination strategy?
4. What other strategies helped you answer the question?

We designed each of these questions to prompt a conversation about particular issues related to decision-making.

How did you feel when you read this question?

If children report that they were worried or anxious about an item, help them explore ways to calm themselves and focus. You might ask other children what they did when a question created anxiety, worry, anger, etc.

Reinforce effective strategies to manage emotions, such as breathing deeply for a moment or two, telling themselves that they are capable and have strategies for problem-solving, or any other technique you have taught children to help them calm down and focus. One teacher taught her students to imagine a tiny helpful person sitting on one shoulder, and a tiny troublemaker on the other. She encouraged them to literally "flick" the troublemaker off their shoulders when the mischief maker gave them negative messages about their abilities. A fourth-grade teacher routinely begins each year with a unit on brain physiology. She helps the children learn about the physical effects of strong emotions on the ability to think and make decisions. During test week, she simply asks them to make sure that they use calming techniques to manage emotions that may flood their thinking abilities.

Other children's performances are affected by overconfidence rather than anxiety or fear. If you notice children rushing through the test, or bragging about how easy the items are, involve them in discussions of items that require reading the directions closely. This procedure may help them to become more careful in their approach to the test.

What did the question ask you to do?

Questions on norm-referenced tests contain crucial key words and signals about the task being required of the children. For each question, you will find suggestions about key words and signals that might help the children more effectively answer questions. *However*, it is important to try to get the children to discover and offer their ideas rather than tell them what they should do.

Could you use the process of elimination strategy?

Although this strategy is not useful for every question, it can help children narrow choices and avoid being distracted by cues the test-maker has deliberately introduced to challenge students to think. Making decisions about what to eliminate depends on reading the questions carefully, recognizing particular subject area cues, and being aware of distracters. You will find information about these issues for each question. Again, students should provide each other with this information through the discussion you will guide. However, if students do not address important cues and signals, you need to bring them to the students' attention.

What other strategies helped you answer the question?

This "catch-all" question gives you and the children an opportunity to acknowledge any other strategies they relied on to help them.

Beginning with Question 23, systematically raise each of these questions. A guide for that conversation follows. With each question, we tried to anticipate and identify common stumbling blocks that might distract children from showing what they know, even if they actually knew the content. The key is to look at test questions through children's eyes. We anticipate that you will have insights that did not occur to us, or to the children and teachers who have helped us think about these questions.

Question 23

1. How did you feel when you read this question?
   - See directions above.
2. What did the question ask you to do?
   - Key words: accurate, perimeters, rectangles
   - This item is difficult because it requires knowledge of both vocabulary and math. If a child doesn't know the meaning of the word "perimeter," he or she should skip the item and return to it if there is time.
   - Use of the abbreviation "cm" may distract some children. In this item, the form of measurement does not matter. In this case, "cm" is *not* a key word; it's a distracter. Tell the children that distracters are like extra information they find in story problems, or in mystery stories or logic problems, where some of the clues are unnecessary. In those situations, the child must figure out what he needs to know or doesn't need to know to solve the problem. Tests contain similar situations. When distracters appear, it's the child's job to figure out which information *distracts* him from what he needs to know to correctly answer the question. We suggest that you talk with the children about being good detectives who must seek out clues.
   - Some children may find the "D" response attractive because only two sides of the rectangles are labeled. They may think they have inadequate information.
3. Could you use the process of elimination strategy? (No)
   - The process of elimination strategy won't work because there is a deliberate visual distracter. One rectangle looks bigger than the other, which would make answer "C" look attractive. Unfortunately, it's wrong. Remind children that occasionally the test-maker will try to divert them from the right answer. In this case, the pictures are deceiving—on purpose.
4. What other strategies helped you answer the question?
   - Work the problem; do the math.

Question 24

1. How did you feel when you read this question?
   - See directions above.
2. What did the question ask you to do?
   - Check to see what children thought the question was asking them to do. Pay particular attention to getting them to describe how they figured out what "diagonally" meant.
   - Key words are "two numbers missing."
3. Could you use the process of elimination strategy? (Yes)
   - Try each pair of numbers. If the first number in the combination doesn't work, go immediately to the next pair.

4. What other strategies helped you answer the question?
  - See what they come up with!

Question 25

1. How did you feel when you read this question?
  - See directions above.
2. What did the question ask you to do?
  - Just remind children to make sure they know whether they're supposed to add, subtract, multiply, or divide.
3. Could you use the process of elimination strategy? (Yes)
  - When time is a factor, subtracting the numbers in the ones place may quickly eliminate a few choices—in this case, the student would know immediately that the answer must have a 4 at the end.
4. What other strategies helped you answer the question?

  - Recognize the little box after the equal sign as a distracter. The box may confuse children, and they may actually write their answer in the box instead of mark their answer sheet. They may think the box is too small for such a big answer. Ask them what they think they're supposed to do with the box. They may come up with some creative responses! Tell them they're not supposed to do anything with the box. It's just a distracter— a cue deliberately introduced by the test-maker to force them to think.
  - Rewrite the problem in a vertical format on a piece of scratch paper.
  - Work the problem and then pick the appropriate answer.

Question 26

1. How did you feel when you read this question?
  - See directions above.
2. What did the question ask you to do?
  - The directions apply only to Questions 26 and 27.
  - The directions say to choose the most accurate response. Even though some children might argue that the bar extends slightly over the "10" marker, it is still closest to "10." If the bar had extended more than halfway over the "10" marker, "12" would have been a better response.
3. Could you use the process of elimination strategy? (Yes)
  - The popcorn bar is obviously higher than "5" or "8," so children could eliminate those two choices.
4. What other strategies helped you answer the question?

  - None that we could think of! The children may have some ideas.

Question 27

1. How did you feel when you read this question?
    - See directions above.
2. What did the question ask you to do?
    - The directions said to use the graph to answer Questions 26 and 27. Children may be tempted to guess at the least favorite snack, based on their own preferences or stereotypes about what fourth-graders might say. Be sure they are working from the information provided.
3. Could you use the process of elimination strategy? (Yes)
    - The bars for popcorn and potato chips are higher than the bar for ice cream. "None of these" doesn't work because the bar for ice cream is the lowest of all four bars.
4. What other strategies helped you answer the question?

    - "None of these" is a distracter that children should choose *only when they are absolutely certain that none of the options are correct.* This seems self-evident, but sometimes children select "none of these" too quickly, without carefully considering all possibilities (they must have put it there for some reason, right?). Standardized tests use different terms to express the idea that the answer has not been provided, such as "NH" for "not here" or "none of the above." Substitute the term used by your state's test.

Question 28

1. How did you feel when you read this question?
    - See directions above.
2. What did the question ask you to do?
    - The word "you" is a distracter in these directions. Children need to know that even if the test-maker uses words like "you," the test-maker is not speaking personally to each person taking the test. So, whether or not *you* use meters is not relevant. This issue becomes even more complicated in state tests that use a combination of extended response and multiple-choice items. In some cases, the extended response items really *do* ask children personally to respond, e.g., "What do you think this poem is about?" If this is the case in your state, alert children to the differences.
    - A key word is "meter." If a child does not know how long a meter is, this question will be very difficult. Remind children to come back to questions they don't know only after they have answered all those they could figure out more easily.
    - Another key word is "would"—as opposed to "could." You *could* measure each of those items in meters, but it's more likely that you *would* measure only one of them.

3. Could you use the process of elimination strategy? (Yes)
   - Students who know how long a meter is should consider each response carefully. "A" is obviously wrong because it would be silly to measure something as small as a finger in meters. "B" makes sense, but is it the best response? Better go on. Most books are smaller than one meter, so we can eliminate "C." What about "D?" "D" is very tempting for children who think the test-maker is speaking personally to them. Back to "B"—the best response.
4. What other strategies helped you answer the question?

   - No others that we could think of, but the children may have some ideas.

Question 29

1. How did you feel when you read this question?
   - See directions above.
2. What did the question ask you to do?
   - Key words are "sum" and "perimeter." If children know what a sum is, and they have read the definition of perimeter, they know what math they need to do.
   - The square is a distracter because of the way it is labeled. A child who didn't read the question carefully might see the numbers and say, "Easy! The sum of $4 + 4 = 8$. The answer must be 'B.'" And they would be wrong.
3. Could you use the process of elimination strategy? (No)
4. What other strategies helped you answer the question?

   - Work the problem and then select the correct answer.
   - Alert children (if they don't raise the issue themselves) that there was a problem earlier in the test that some may have skipped because they didn't know the definition of perimeter. Occasionally, although not frequently, information in one question may help to answer another question. Remind them to stay alert. In this case, look back at Question 23.

This concludes the review of the practice test on this day. Collect the answer sheets and test booklets. Add new strategies to strategy chart.

Script

"Good job! I'm delighted to see how well you are thinking. You are developing some excellent decision-making strategies. Let's add any new strategies to our chart. Tomorrow, we will finish going over the test."

Remember to chart strategies.

CHAPTER ELEVEN

Workshop Seven
Thinking Like a Detective

One of the teachers who worked with these materials gave us the idea of using the metaphor of thinking inside and outside the box. He explained to his students that thinking inside the box was to think like the test-maker. As his students worked through the questions, they would sometimes explain their responses by saying, "Well, if I were thinking outside the box, I might argue for this answer because . . ." An imaginative and creatively logical response might follow. Then they would continue, "But if I were thinking inside the box, I'd go with this other answer because . . . ," and would cite a response more attuned to the logic of adult thinking. Perhaps this manner of framing the differences in the kinds of thinking needed on some test questions would work with your students as well.

You've almost made it! This is the last workshop prior to the actual test. You can either follow the same structure we outlined for day six, or you can proceed in a more open-ended way. A more open-ended approach would involve systematically going through the remaining six items of Practice Test 2 and asking simply, "What strategies did you use to help yourself figure out the answer to this question?"

To give you maximum flexibility to decide what to do on this last day, we have used the same four-question structure to describe the strategies. If you elect the open-ended approach, you can still use the information to enhance your conversation with the students.

Step 1: Review the Last Six Items of Practice Test 2.

Script
"Today we're going to finish going over the items on the practice test that we didn't get to yesterday. This is the last day we're going to work on these strategies before you take the test, so let's try to pull together everything you've learned.

"Let's start with a quick review. You have been working hard for six days to learn effective problem-solving strategies that will help you with the upcoming tests. But, do you know something? Some of these strategies will also help you whenever you encounter unfamiliar situations. Let's review just a few of them.

"First, when you encounter an unfamiliar situation that makes you worried or anxious, what do you need to do?" *ELICIT IDEAS ABOUT SELF-CALMING STRATEGIES.*

"Once you feel ready to explore the situation, what do you need to do?" *TRY TO GET THEM TO SAY THAT THEY NEED TO FIGURE OUT WHAT THE NEW SITUATION REQUIRES THEM TO DO. YOU MIGHT USE THE EXAMPLE OF SITTING DOWN AT A COMPUTER FOR THE FIRST TIME. THEY HAVE TO REALIZE THAT THE FIRST THING THEY HAVE TO DO IS FIGURE OUT HOW TO TURN THE COMPUTER ON.*

"And once you know what the situation requires you to do, how do you figure out how to proceed?" *TRY TO GET THEM TO TELL YOU THAT THEY WOULD TRY TO IDENTIFY PROBLEM-SOLVING STRATEGIES THAT WOULD WORK IN THE SITUATION. FOR INSTANCE, IF YOU USED THE COMPUTER EXAMPLE, ASK THEM WHAT PROBLEM-SOLVING STRATEGIES THEY WOULD USE TO FIGURE OUT HOW TO TURN THE COMPUTER ON.*

"Good work! I'm really impressed with what you have learned. Let's go over these last six test items."

DISTRIBUTE THE TEST BOOKLETS AND ANSWER SHEETS.

REVIEW QUESTIONS 30–35, USING EITHER THE STRUCTURED APPROACH MODELED IN THE WORKSHOP ON DAY SIX, OR THE MORE OPEN-ENDED APPROACH DESCRIBED IN THE INTRODUCTION TO TODAY'S WORKSHOP.

REMEMBER, THE PURPOSE IS TO TRY TO HELP THE CHILDREN DISCOVER AND OFFER IDEAS, RATHER THAN TELL THEM WHAT THEY SHOULD DO. REFER BACK TO THE GENERAL INSTRUCTIONS FOR LEADING THE DISCUSSION OUTLINED AT THE BEGINNING OF THE WORKSHOP ON DAY SIX.

Question 30

1. How did you feel when you read this question?
2. What did the question ask you to do?
   - This is a division problem.
   - Students in states that permit the use of calculators during tests may need to practice translating the mathematical language of decimals into the language of "remainders."
3. Could you use the process of elimination strategy? (No)
4. What other strategies helped you answer this question?
   - Write the problem on a piece of scratch paper and work it out before looking for the answer in the list.
   - Here's an occasion when "none of the above" is actually the correct response. It's a good reminder to do the math.

Question 31

1. How did you feel when you read this question?
2. What did the question ask you to do?
   - The directions say to choose the best answer to complete the sentence. Be sure children understand that the line indicates where the answer would go in the sentence.
   - Key words are "last night" because they give a clue to the timing of this action.
   - The name Raitha may be a distracter, as some children may get stuck trying to pronounce the name in their minds. Tell them they can substitute any name if it will help them to more easily read the question.
3. Could you use the process of elimination strategy? (Yes)
   - Children can eliminate answers "A" ("break") and "C" ("will break") because the key words suggest that the action took place in the past. That narrows the selection to two possibilities.
4. What other strategies helped you answer the question?
   - Suggest that they *predict* what word might make sense in the sentence before they read all the possible responses.

Question 32

1. How did you feel when you read this question?
2. What did the question ask you to do?
   - This is a spelling item.
3. Could you use the process of elimination strategy? (Yes)
   - Children can eliminate answer "B." Although it is correctly spelled, it doesn't make sense in the context of the sentence.
4. What other strategies helped you answer the question?
   - There are three strategies that may help children with spelling items. The first is to create a mental picture. Suggest that the children close their eyes and try to imagine how to spell the word, and then look for that spelling in the list. Although they must glance at the list of words to know which word they're supposed to spell, staring at the list may be confusing; sometimes misspellings begin to look correct.
   - Another hint is to write the word on a piece of scratch paper the way they think it is spelled. If children don't have scratch paper, they can use their fingers to write the word invisibly on the desk.
   - Often, although it is not true of this item because of the homophone, children do not need to read the sentence in which the spelling word is omitted. Instead, children can go directly to the response and simply choose the word that is spelled correctly. Obviously, as this question illustrates, this strategy must be used judiciously, but it may save time for both good and poor readers.

Question 33

1. How did you feel when you read this question?
2. What did the question ask you to do?
   - Key words are "most likely" and "large." Although some children may argue that they can find a map of Spain in any of the places listed, the most accurate response for a "large" and "most likely" location is "atlas."
   - Once again, the word "you" is a distracter. The test-maker is not talking personally to a child. It doesn't matter if someone would most likely find the large map of Spain in a nifty software package on the school library's computer. Their only choices are those listed here and the test-maker thinks one is better than the rest. The students' job is to figure out the clues that will lead them to the answer the test-maker has chosen—the most accurate answer.
3. Could you use the process of elimination strategy? (Yes)
   - Children could eliminate "dictionary" because the pictures in a dictionary are usually very small. Almanacs generally contain calendars of information, not maps of countries. Encyclopedias are tempting because they do contain maps, but the key word clue, "most likely" would lead a good sleuth to the "atlas" response.
4. What other strategies helped you answer the question?
   - None that we could think of!

Question 34

1. How did you feel when you read the question?
2. What did the question ask you to do?
   - The directions say to find the sentence that would fit in the paragraph where the line is. That means children need to think about the sequence of actions that the paragraph is describing.
3. Could you use the process of elimination strategy? (Yes)
   - Children can eliminate "A" because it's not a sentence. They can eliminate "C" because Taylor already had her gloves on. "D" can be eliminated because it would occur only after she planted the seeds. That leaves "B."
4. What other strategies helped you answer the question?
   - None that we could think of!

Question 35

1. How did you feel when you read the question?
2. What did the question ask you to do?
   - A key word is "opinion."
   - The directions say to read the story to answer Question 35.

- The name Amelia Earhart may be a distracter. Although many children may have heard the name spoken before, some may get stuck trying to pronounce the name in their minds. Remind them they can substitute any name if it will help them to more easily read the story.

3. Could you use the process of elimination strategy? (Yes)
   - If you know the difference between a fact and an opinion, you could eliminate responses "A," "B," and "C."

4. What other strategies helped you answer the question?
   - A general strategy children should be aware of is to read the question before reading the story. The question will give them a clue as to what to look for while they are reading.
   - In this case, even though the directions say to read the story to answer the question, a child who knew the difference between a fact and an opinion could actually answer the question without reading the story.

END ON AN UPBEAT NOTE, CONGRATULATING THE CHILDREN FOR THEIR HARD WORK AND NEW DECISION-MAKING SKILLS. INVITE THEM TO ADD ANY FINAL STRATEGIES TO THE STRATEGY CHART AND DO A QUICK REVIEW OF THE STRATEGIES LISTED ON THE CHART.

COLLECT THE TEST BOOKLETS AND ANSWER SHEETS.

This is the last workshop prior to administration of the test. There is one more workshop after the test to give the children an opportunity to talk about the experience of taking the test, and to elicit their reactions in writing through a posttest survey.

CHAPTER TWELVE

Workshop Eight

Assessing Students' Experiences and Reactions

Amanda was literally dancing in her seat. Her glee was impossible to contain. She knew that she was going to finish this section of the test, and she obviously felt confident she was doing well. Her teacher shook her head in amazement. This was the same student whose anxiety prior to the test had been sky high. Amanda had traveled a long way.

Stories like these, and a growing collection of data, persuade us that these workshops have a positive impact on children. But you can assess that for yourself. We recommend that you elicit students' stories and experiences in two ways. First, get the children to complete the posttest survey, "So, What Did You Think?" Second, lead a whole-group discussion.

Step 1: Complete the Posttest Survey.

As soon as possible after the children have completed the tests, ask them to complete the survey, "So, What Did You Think?" As you did with the pretest survey, read the items aloud to the students. Collect the surveys, and for your own information, compare them to the pretest surveys.

Step 2: Lead a Whole-Group Discussion.

The discussion is an opportunity for the children to talk about the experience of taking the test. Just a few simple questions will give them a chance to share their thoughts and give you an opportunity to hear what the experience was like for them. We suggest the following questions:

1. What was interesting (enjoyable, fun, challenging—choose a positive descriptor) about taking the tests?
2. What was surprising or difficult about the tests?
3. If you were going to try to help next year's class get ready for this test, what advice would you give them?

CHAPTER THIRTEEN

Stories from the Front

The Ethics and Practice of Test Preparation

It was a dark and stormy night (really!). We had been driving for five hours and had almost arrived at our destination. We were tired, hungry, and regretful that we had driven by the last rest stop; it wasn't the best time to discover we were lost. We struggled to maintain our sense of humor. Since we were on the road to conduct one of our test preparation training sessions with teachers, we facetiously turned to the four strategies we recommend for approaching unfamiliar test items and applied them to our plight. What do you know? It worked!

"Manage your emotions!"

"Figure out what you are being asked to do!"

"Begin with what you know!"

"Narrow the possibilities!"

Managing our emotions meant we had to push through the grouchiness and frustration of finding ourselves in this situation at nine o'clock at night. *Figuring out what we needed to do* was simple—we needed to find our hotel. We *began with what we knew* about number sequences. We had passed exits 2, 3, and 4. Because we were looking for exit 5, we assumed we were headed in the right direction. Imagine our consternation when we saw that the next exit was numbered 1, clear evidence that this highway was not using the numbering system rules that we knew. We quickly *narrowed our options* to two: leaving the freeway and reentering in the opposite direction, or getting off the freeway and stopping for directions so we could wend our way through town. (Okay, so we considered getting off the freeway and finding the nearest restaurant that sold hot fudge sundaes, but just for a fleeting moment.) We chose the second option and successfully located the hotel.

We laugh about that incident now, and use the story to illustrate that you really can transfer some of the skills needed to negotiate a norm-referenced, multiple-choice test to daily life. Or put another way, *some of the skills we use to approach unfamiliar situations can help us take norm-referenced tests.*

In the latter part of this chapter, we will explore the possibility of integrating test preparation principles, formats, and skills into the curriculum so that they become a familiar part of the students' routine. Through excerpts of interviews that we conducted with teachers, we will offer authentic ideas that may help spur your thinking or confirm your own practices.

Ethics and Test Preparation

Before we enter into this discussion, however, we want to come full-circle to the ethical issues we raised in the first chapter. Preeminent among them are two questions: What test preparation practices are ethical? How can teachers integrate these ethical practices into their curriculum? (For other authors' descriptions of ethical practices, see Mehrens and Kaminski 1989, 114–122; Popham 1995; and Smith 1991, 521–542.)

A teacher friend of ours underscored the importance of returning to the first question when she confided that she realized only recently that she could look at the items on her students' standardized test. She had assumed that looking at the items was a breach of ethics, although when pressed, she couldn't really say why. She told us that in her experience, teachers spent little time talking about this "stuff," and suggested it would be helpful to specify acceptable and unacceptable teacher practices. She admitted,

> I simply was not informed. What's more, I didn't want to be informed. And I definitely wasn't motivated to figure out what was ethical practice. I couldn't see the value of the test for my students. I felt really conflicted because my preference is to run a student-centered classroom, and when you do that, the paths you go down might not match up with a standardized test. But at the same time, I felt administrators were telling me that if I were really a good teacher, all my students would do well on the test. I couldn't resolve this conflict between what I thought was being a good teacher, and what external messages were saying about the importance of standardized test scores. It was a heavy guilt trip, and I dealt with it by avoiding the issue. I had a bad attitude, was sloppy, and wanted the whole mess to just go away.

The literature suggests that our friend's attitudes and confusion are not uncommon. We took her advice, and offer our answers to questions about ethical practices.

Questions That Are Best Answered, "No, Don't Go There"
Is it okay for me to:

1. duplicate questions from the norm-referenced test used in my school for students to practice? *No.*
2. provide hints about or rephrase test items? *No.*
3. provide correct answers? *No.*
4. alter marks on answer sheets? *No.*
5. tell children that the tests don't matter? *No.*
6. do nothing to prepare children for norm-referenced tests? *No.*

We assume you know that the answers to Questions 1 through 4 are "no," but in an era when teachers and administrators are under tremendous pressure to raise test scores, it doesn't hurt to state definitively that in the profession of education, these are considered unacceptable practices. Individuals may rationalize their decision to use these practices because they believe that extenuating circumstances such as inequities in resource allocation for students, disagreement with the ways in which test scores are used, or concern about students' self-esteem justify their actions. But to paraphrase the immortal words of Richard Nixon, let's make this point perfectly clear: If you engage in these practices, it's considered cheating.

Conversely, Questions 5 and 6 refer to the ethics of responsibility, and we raise them because they are at the heart of this book. We believe, as do many teachers, that children deserve equitable access to educational opportunities. Since norm-referenced tests are often the gates to opportunities, it is unethical to cause children to dismiss the importance of these tests, or to leave them unprepared to adequately reveal their knowledge.

Questions That Are Best Answered, "It Depends . . ."
In this gray area, your actions could be either ethical or unethical. We explain why in the discussion that follows each question.

7. Is it okay for me to look at the items on my students' standardized tests? *It depends on your purpose.* You are on ethically firm ground if you are informing yourself about how the test assesses children's knowledge, and what knowledge is included in the assessment. Teachers need to be able to answer parents' questions about the meaning of test scores. They need to know what is implied when a test report states, for example, "Students need to work on punctuation." Unless you know the form and content of the questions used to assess an area of knowledge, you will not know how to interpret scores for yourself and for parents. Teachers also need to be able to analyze the reasons for discrepancies between norm-referenced test scores and classroom assessments. Again, without knowledge of the test questions, this evaluation would be incomplete.

On the other hand, if you were looking at the items for the purpose of duplicating them for practice, your actions would be considered unethical.

8. Is it okay for me to teach to the test? *It depends on whether your standardized test is norm- or criterion-referenced.* Teaching to the test generally means providing instruction on objectives matched to the test and practicing the same format as the test questions. Purists would argue that this practice is inappropriate, regardless of whether the test is norm- or criterion-referenced. They reason that items on both types of tests generally *sample* the domain of knowledge being assessed, and adequately represent a broader construct of achievement. In order to draw valid inferences about that achievement (and not simply about students' knowledge and skill on the specific items tested), students should not experience "teaching to the test."

Others would argue that purists don't live in the real world of classrooms and school politics. They would assert that if what the test measures is important, teachers should teach to it. However, some would draw distinctions between the two types of standardized tests. On a criterion-referenced test, items generally reflect clear, specific, and public objectives that have preset standards (criteria) against which student performance is judged. Teachers and students know what students are expected to achieve and what level of performance is considered acceptable. Theoretically, "all" students could potentially meet the standard. In this case, it is not only ethical to "teach to the test," but teachers are *expected* to teach to it when the objectives of the test align with state and district curricula.

By contrast, a norm-referenced test judges student performance against the performance of a norm group, and test-makers expect achievement to follow the "normal distribution." Teachers who focus their instruction on test items risk "skewing" (distorting) the normal distribution. Furthermore, districts that respond to accountability pressures by bringing their curricula in closer alignment with the test risk the same result. As the curricula more closely approximate the knowledge domains of a published test, scores rise. When scores rise enough, test companies renorm the test and/or change the test content. Districts must then readjust their curricula or rise to the public relations challenge presented by lower scores. Although some educators would argue that there is nothing wrong with nationally standardized tests dictating local curriculum (again, if what the test measures is important, why not teach to it?), others would object strenuously. The degree to which district and state curricula align with their norm-referenced tests varies considerably. For instance, within the last decade, Arizona discovered that only "about 26 percent of the state's objectives were tested by the most closely aligned test," prompting a restructuring of its assessment system (Nolan, Haladyna, and Haas 1992).

9. Is it okay for me to read the questions to a student during the test? *It depends on what the test is measuring.* If you were reading questions to a student on a test that is designed to measure reading comprehension, your actions would be inappropriate. If you were reading questions to a student on a test designed to measure a subject other than reading, you would be on more solid ground. Test administration guidelines usually address these issues and recommend standardized procedures.

Two groups of students deserve mention. Some students will have Individualized Educational Plans (IEPs) that clearly stipulate any special accommodations that are appropriate. If you work with children with IEPs, we strongly recommend that you check to be sure that suitable accommodations for taking norm-referenced tests have been included.

For teachers who work with students for whom English is a second language, we urge you to ask if there is a version of the test in the student's language or if translators can assist students. One of the purposes of standardized achievement tests is to determine what children know. Research on second language acquisition clearly demonstrates that it takes a minimum of five years to gain enough facility in a second language for a student to adequately represent her knowledge (Thomas and Collier 1998). Although testing in a student's first language is not common, it *is* ethical. If neither a translated test nor translators are available, advocate strongly that these children be exempted from testing until their English has developed sufficiently to accurately portray their knowledge. If you find these doors are closed, work hard to ensure that someone reads the nonreading sections of the test to the children. After the test, advocate equally hard for the test company to report the child's test scores in the parents' first language.

Two ethical issues are at stake here. It is indefensible to evaluate children's knowledge when their language skills are not sufficiently developed to reveal that knowledge. However, it is equally indefensible to test children in their first language and then discount those scores for reporting purposes. Teachers in one southwestern state shared with us that the school district reported the scores of Spanish-speaking children who took their norm-referenced test in English. However, the reports excluded the scores of Spanish-speaking children who took the test in Spanish (the majority of students in that school), even though the children performed well. This policy sends a clear message to children about who and what counts, and provides inaccurate information to the public about children's capabilities.

10. Is it okay for me to provide extra time on timed portions of the test? *It depends on whether students have IEPs that permit a special accommodation of this nature, or if test directions allow extra time for ESL students.* If not, it is unethical to extend time limits.
11. Is it okay for me to exclude some of my students from taking the test or their scores from being included in the report of school performance? *It depends on your district's policies.* Please see the response to question nine.

Questions That Are Best Answered, "Yes, Absolutely"
Is it okay for me to:

12. teach test-taking skills? *Yes.*
13. teach children language commonly associated with tests, e.g., terms like multiple-choice, distracter, one best answer, answer (bubble) sheet, test booklet, etc.? *Yes.*
14. teach children how to reduce stress and manage their emotions? *Yes.*
15. encourage students to get lots of sleep and show up during test week? *Yes.*
16. leave a list of student-generated test preparation strategies posted in the room? *Yes.*

In order to design the workshops in Chapters Five through Twelve, we needed to resolve for ourselves the ethical issues raised in all sixteen of these questions. Our conviction that the responses to these last five questions were unequivocally "yes" influenced the content and structure of the workshops.

Making Test Strategies Part of Your Classroom Curriculum

We firmly believe that teachers have a responsibility to prepare children to show what they know on *all* forms of assessment, including norm-referenced tests. We also know that our workshops are an ethical and effective avenue for accomplishing this purpose. Research (including our own) suggests that elementary school children *do* benefit from preparation focused on test-taking skills (Scruggs, White, and Bennion 1986). But we are not convinced that a stand-alone test preparation unit *only* offered immediately prior to a high-stakes assessment is the best choice. It makes sense to us that the strategies needed in test-taking would be better learned if they were part of daily curriculum, and then reinforced by our workshops just prior to the test.

The suggestions that follow for integrating principles and strategies of test-taking supplement the formal workshops. We intended these approaches to help children develop an understanding of themselves as learners and to begin building the skills needed for test-taking. *Most of these strategies could be adapted to any elementary grade level.*

But I Teach Primary Grades—Am I Off the Hook?

When we began conducting our workshops in schools, primary teachers often asked us how to help younger students prepare for tests. Some asked because they agreed test preparation should be a whole-school responsibility. Others faced the reality that in their districts, norm-referenced testing began in first grade. We question the appropriateness of our workshops for younger children, and assessing their knowledge using norm-referenced tests. We base our reservations in part on recommendations made by the National Association for the Education of Young Children (1988) about developmentally appropriate practices. Nevertheless, many states assess primary-age children using norm-referenced tests. Because we target our workshop materials for children in grades three through six, we think that primary teachers will find this next section to be particularly helpful.

General Approaches for Integrating Test Preparation into All Elementary Classes

Remember the story in the first chapter about the child who didn't know she had it in her to ride a bike? Many children aren't aware of "what they have in them" that could help them as learners. Theories of cognitive development, however, suggest that learning is enhanced when the learner is able to step back and reflect on the processes of learning, as well as the content. Unfortunately, the burden of escalating curriculum requirements often steers teachers' attention toward the details of content. There is little time for helping children understand the hows and whys of their unique learning processes, and the demands of various types of cognitive tasks. But it can be done. Teachers can easily fold strategies for helping children understand their emotional reactions and effective and ineffective approaches to academic tasks into daily lessons. These strategies serve a dual purpose. They help children learn new skills and they help teachers assess what their students feel, know, and can do. Each assessment can inform teaching practices. As one teacher commented:

> I think it's just as wrong to suddenly plunk kids into a test situation without having exposed them to what they need to know and do to be successful on the test, as it is to put a book, cold turkey, in front of a kid who's just learning to read. Working on the strategies all year is *not* teaching to the test. Your workshop materials helped the kids but they *really* helped *me* hear the kids' questions so I could decide how to work with the strategies. I could see from the strategies what the kids would be asked to do on tests, and how I could plug the strategies into everyday practices all year, so that we could just review right before the test.

Strategies for identifying and managing emotional responses

Children's emotions affect their learning. Teachers can encourage children to recognize how their feelings help or get in the way of their learning through straightforward strategies such as these.

- Deliberately introduce activities that will challenge the comfort level of your students. Learning does not occur without a balance of challenge and support. Further, what is easy for one child is challenging for another. Too much challenge provokes feelings of worry or concern, and too much support interferes with a child's willingness to take the risk that learning entails. To help balance challenge and support when you introduce new learning experiences, take time to let the students discuss what they think they are being asked to do, how they feel, and how they plan to proceed.

    One third/fourth-grade teacher addresses this issue through regularly sharing with her students specific stories of her reactions and responses to new things that she's learning. She feels that her honesty encourages her students to discuss their feelings more freely and to work with them. For example, she is learning to play the guitar. Even though she feels anxious about performing in front of people, she accompanies the children when they sing. By letting them know that she is a little nervous, she helps the children see that it's possible to manage feelings that might interfere with new experiences. Over time, these types of conversations may become a "habit of mind" that will build positive self-talk into all sorts of new learning situations, including norm-referenced tests.

- Provide frequent opportunities through group discussions for students to share how they feel *after* new or unfamiliar activities. Create a visual record of the children's responses by writing their "before" and "after" reactions to new learning experiences on a chart. This way you and the children can assess changes in their responses over time.

- Explore the language of feelings with children. Many children have limited vocabulary to express the range of their feelings, and may benefit from being able to express themselves more accurately. Using pictures or photographs to elicit conversations about feelings can expand children's vocabularies and increase teachers' understandings of their students. This knowledge may help teachers support students in challenging situations, including norm-referenced tests.

    Another simple way to encourage students to name and talk about their emotional responses to classroom work is to add statements to any worksheet like, "I felt _____ when solving this problem. This feeling helped me/got in my way (choose one). So I _____." It is as important to talk with the children about these statements as it is for the students to complete them.

■ Identify major transitions (e.g., riding the bus, buying hot lunch, becoming part of the school orchestra, qualifying for the school patrol, experiencing in-school health exams, moving to middle school) in children's school lives that are likely to cause stress and anxiety, and build these into your curriculum. This strategy will serve two purposes. First, transitions are significant, and they compel your students' attention. They are ready-made events that can give rise to authentic learning experiences. If you ignore those transitions, students may be distracted from other things you have planned. Second, you can use these existing events to meet curriculum objectives and help children learn to identify and effectively manage their emotions to enhance learning. Such mini-units can help students identify effective strategies they use to manage the emotions that arise when they confront new situations. *These strategies are unlikely to be generalized unless the teacher deliberately and explicitly guides the students in understanding that these skills will transfer to other new situations, including norm-referenced tests.*

For example, a fourth/fifth-grade teacher incorporates a unit on transition to middle school into her curriculum. She begins by eliciting the children's expectations, fears, and anxieties. Then she provides opportunities for them to ask questions, conduct their own research, and gather information from middle school teachers, counselors, and former elementary school students. Learning experiences range from practicing the skill of opening lockers with combination locks to taking field trips to middle school. Journals provide students with opportunities to share their feelings and receive feedback from their teachers and peers. In focus groups, children describe situations that are real or that they fear, such as not having friends, and then cooperatively imagine attitudes and actions that are more likely to get them what they want. This teacher and others we spoke with stressed the importance of actively converting children's negative self-talk to more positive behaviors through whole-group and individual conversation. One offered this advice:

> When you're working with kids about unfamiliar situations and emotions, you have to establish that it's okay to share feelings. Whenever a child offers something to you, no matter how ridiculous, try to take it seriously, regardless of what you think the child's motives are. I listen no matter what.

■ Introduce strategies to help children cope with feelings of anxiety, anger, frustration, and boredom/indifference. These may be strategies that you suggest (e.g., breathing exercises; relaxing muscles in the shoulders and face; making it okay to express feelings out loud; positive self-talk—saying to yourself, "I can do this"; counting to ten; etc.) or they may be strategies that children offer. Be sure to give children the opportunity to volunteer strategies they use to calm themselves. Don't forget to talk about the dangers of overconfidence as well.

Integrating strategies that encourage reflection about learning

Four strategies that are helpful for approaching unfamiliar test items are also quite useful when approaching any new learning situation. In addition to managing their emotions, children need to figure out what is being asked of them, determine what they already know, and narrow down their options to form a plan. These strategies require children to actively reflect upon their learning processes, a skill that needs to be systematically nurtured in the classroom. Here are sample strategies for helping your students develop that skill.

- Give children ample practice reading, writing, and giving and interpreting directions and test questions. A great place to start is with a jar of peanut butter, a loaf of bread, and a knife. If you've never tried this activity, it's quite useful in providing children with insights about how to make sense of directions. Here's how you do it. Put your peanut butter, loaf of bread, and knife on a table and ask your students to give you directions for making your peanut butter sandwich. Often, children will begin by saying, "Put the peanut butter on the bread." You should do just that—place the unopened jar of peanut butter on top of the unopened loaf of bread and react expressively—look puzzled, triumphant, etc. Of course, your students will groan and say, "No! No! The peanut butter has to go on the bread!" Your job is to continue acting out their instructions *literally*. For example, when they tell you to open the jar, you should turn the jar upside down, look confused, perhaps twist the cap the wrong way or attempt to pry it open with the knife. Eventually, the children will become more precise in their directions and the sandwich *will* get made.

  The follow-up conversation could go many ways. However, for the purpose of connecting this activity to norm-referenced tests, you might focus on what to do when directions are unclear, or make assumptions about what the learner already knows. If you have a practice version of your norm-referenced test, you could ask students to work in pairs, examine a set of directions, and then explain to another pair what they think the directions are asking. Children can write or give oral directions for other children to follow as extensions of this activity. These types of experiences sharpen students' abilities to correctly ascertain the technical demands of different kinds of directions.

- Provide regular opportunities for children to discuss approaches to their work. One primary, multigrade teacher, who organizes her classroom around centers, helps children develop the habit of explaining their work through her individual conversations with them. After each child finishes a center, she routinely asks, "What did you do at this center? How did you get that answer? Why did you do it that way? What were you asked to do? What was going on in your mind when you were trying to solve that problem? What was helping you decide what to do?" During these conversations she points out key words and phrases that help children learn how to "get meaning" from what they have read. When children misunderstand directions, or insist that they can't get it, or can't do it, she asks them to read the directions out loud, or read the directions to themselves and rephrase them out loud for her. In this way, children practice individually strategies that she has presented to the whole class. Behaviors such as rephrasing directions and reflecting on the learning process become habits that support the children when they take tests or encounter new learning situations. During actual tests, this teacher has found that children need only simple reminders about figuring out directions, or focusing on what they're being asked to do to encourage them to easily slip into habits they have developed over the year.

A third/fourth-grade teacher who spoke about the importance of acknowledging and naming the strategies children already have gave us another example of a way to provide opportunities for children to discuss approaches to their work. Frequently, children have well-developed strategies but don't realize it until the teacher points out what the child is doing and why it is useful. For example, sometimes young children don't realize that reading ahead to gather clues that will help them figure out an unknown word is a good strategy until the teacher legitimizes it. Children have similar misperceptions about what strategies may be permissible in a norm-referenced test. Teachers should explicitly connect children's effective problem-solving strategies that arise in classroom conversations with strategies that are useful on norm-referenced tests (see Chapters Ten and Eleven for specific ideas).

A third approach was offered by a middle school teacher who uses rubrics to help his students determine what they already know about a unit of study and then develop plans for their individual projects. The outcomes of the unit are clearly specified but he encourages students to design their own projects and presentations based on the expectations detailed in the rubrics. Once the students have developed their plans, they meet with the teacher to explain their decisions and discuss approaches to their work.

■ Use strategies to reinforce decision-making steps. "KWL," shorthand for "What do we know?" "What do we want to learn?" "What have we learned?", is an example of this type of strategy. Many teachers introduce new units of study by asking their students to brainstorm everything they already "know" about the subject. This brainstormed list, written under the "K" on a chart, may include both accurate and inaccurate knowledge. Teachers then ask children what they want to learn about the new topic, and write these questions under the "W." The questions serve as a focus for children's investigations. During and after the unit, the teacher and children return to the chart to assess what has been learned. They modify original ideas and add new information under the "L." For teachers who use "KWL," a simple adaptation focused on multiple-choice formats might be useful for children in third grade or above.

In this variation, the teacher writes a multiple-choice question with possible responses on the board. He asks children what the question asks them to do (e.g., write a number sentence, find the closest estimate, choose the word with the opposite meaning, etc.). He charts their ideas under "K." Then, for the "W" column, students brainstorm what they need to do to narrow the possible choices (see Chapters Nine, Ten, and Eleven for useful strategies). Finally, as they discuss their approaches to answering the questions, the teacher records under the "L" what the students learned about themselves and multiple-choice questions. You can increase the benefits of using "KWL" in this way if you use and discuss a variety of question formats and content.

Integrating strategies that provide practice with common formats, test language, and timed conditions

The format of a standardized test is foreign to most children's (and adults'!) experience of everyday life. Yet, if you think about a test simply as a different way of presenting written material—not unlike a recipe, poem, fairy tale, or sign—you can help children become adept at understanding how to successfully engage this format. Specifically, children need to understand that there are multiple ways of presenting problems and questions. For example, if teachers present addition problems only in a vertical format, or use only the phrase "number sentence" to describe an equation, children may be caught off-guard when they encounter different presentations or terms on a norm-referenced test. Children also need to understand that each question on a multiple-choice test has only one acceptable answer. Finally, they need to become accustomed to working alone, and in many states, under timed conditions.

To familiarize children with formats used in standardized tests, you might incorporate these different ways of presenting materials in your regular teaching. *Just including them is insufficient, however.* It's important that you name the differences and let the children talk about their reactions and strategies for answering the questions. Your goal is to "normalize" the experience of multiple-choice tests. Below are several examples of ways to accomplish this goal.

- Provide students with experiences in using both vertical and horizontal presentations of math problems, different symbols that indicate algorithms, and synonyms such as "equation" for "number sentence." Let's look at just one example.

$$3 + 3 = \qquad \text{vs.} \qquad \begin{array}{r} 3 \\ + 3 \\ \hline \end{array}$$

In a discussion about these two different presentations, you might say: "Math problems may be written in both of these ways. How many of you prefer to work the math problem when it's written horizontally (side to side)? How many of you prefer to work the math problem when it's written vertically (up and down)? What makes you like one way better than the other?" Then you could matter-of-factly note that it's okay to rewrite the problem the way they find it easier to work. You're legitimizing different approaches and preferences, and you're normalizing the presentation of math problems.

- Model for children what it means to choose only one "right" or "best" answer among limited choices. It isn't unusual these days to ask children to make predictions about stories, talk about what they liked or didn't like, retell the major components in the story, or speculate about other possible solutions, endings, etc. In math teachers often ask them to develop conceptual understandings by working with manipulatives and creating ways to solve problems. So children may not understand that it is possible to respond to a piece of writing or a math problem by choosing one right or best answer from a predetermined list. However, standardized tests require that children understand the assumption that one "right" answer exists for each question presented to them.

Schools that use "Daily Oral Language" (DOL) may find this task to be a natural setting for encouraging children to practice the skill of locating one right answer. Once a week you could write your DOL sentence on the board followed by restricted choices. For example:

susan[1] lives in Olympia, Washington[2]

1. a. Susan
   b. susan
   c. SuSan
   d. SUSAN

2. a. ,
   b. ?
   c. .
   d. "

Ask children to work alone to select the correct responses and record their answers on a bubble sheet. Talk with them about this new format and encourage them to share their reasons for selecting particular answers. Only after this discussion has taken place, tell them which is the "right" or "best" answer, and lead a discussion about why this answer is best. Eventually, children will become aware that this format signals a particular way of responding *and* they will become more adept with grammatical conventions. Teachers have adapted the DOL strategy for geography and to report classroom "Daily News." You could easily adapt this strategy to some of your math lessons, also.

■ Give children practice with questions that ask for opinions and questions that ask for information based on a particular reading passage. On norm-referenced tests and in some reading series, questions may be phrased in such a way that children assume they are being asked for their opinion instead of a "right" answer. For example, one test item provided a short "story" followed by five questions. The last question asked, "What will many deer probably do next summer?" Some children, particularly younger children, will not naturally maintain the story's perspective when a question is framed like this. They are quite likely to select the answer that most closely fits their own notions about what the deer will do!

   Therefore, we would encourage you to regularly (but not constantly!) include in your book discussions questions that may seem to be asking a personal opinion but that are really asking about information in, or inferences based on, the text. We'd also encourage you to present these questions orally and in written form using the selected choice format. Again, simply including new questions is not sufficient. It's the regular discussions you have with your students about *why* they provided particular answers that will help them understand how to respond to this type of question.

■ Invent ways for children to use multiple-choice formats authentically. One middle school teacher, for example, involves his students in creating written assessments for each of their units of study. He provides models for the kinds of questions he feels are important, teaches the students how to write multiple-choice and true/false questions, and engages them in discussions about what in the unit is important to be assessed.

   A fourth/fifth-grade teacher suggested another way she could easily integrate multiple-choice formats into something she was already doing. She begins her class each day with a "wake-up" exercise. When her students enter the room, they know to look at the board or the overhead for the problem of the day. She presents these problems, drawn from minute mysteries, logic puzzle books, supplements to the school's math series, and children's magazines, in a variety of formats, including multiple-choice. Students work alone or with partners and then discuss how they solved the problems.

This teacher acknowledged that she had not explicitly connected "wake-up" work with strategies that would be effective on norm-referenced tests. After our conversation, however, she became excited about making these connections and could easily cite resources that would be readily available for this purpose.

Two elementary teachers offered the following suggestions. A third/fourth-grade teacher who uses centers thought it would be easy to add a center focused on test preparation. She envisioned using minilessons to introduce the skills included in the center. A second teacher who works with parent volunteers described one way that she integrates multiple-choice formats to provide opportunities for her students to increase their understanding of tests. The children take practice tests individually and then discuss their answers and strategies in small groups with a trained parent volunteer.

■ Give students practice working alone, and if typical of your state test, under timed conditions. We provided several examples of ways teachers give children practice "working alone" in Chapter Four. Here we would like to reiterate the importance of "normalizing" the process of working under timed conditions. One teacher described a creative use of sand timers that students built for a unit on time. She gently introduced children to the experience of being timed by encouraging them to use their timers to see how quickly they can perform a task. While it is important for children to have experiences like these before a test, it is equally important to offer these experiences in developmentally appropriate ways.

Keeping Children at the Center

Like many educators reading this book, we know that well-developed, classroom-based authentic assessments are essential for informing teachers about what their students know and need to learn. We believe that these kinds of assessments are better indicators of individual students' knowledge and growth than nationally normed, standardized tests. We know that many teachers do not believe that norm-referenced tests add to their understanding of their students' academic accomplishments. When children do not understand how to accurately demonstrate their knowledge on norm-referenced tests, we agree with this critique. However, children *can* learn to negotiate these tests and teachers *can* use the process of test preparation to learn about how their students reason and make meaning. In a world where assessment has taken on "mythic" proportions, it is incumbent upon educators to help children develop the skills and attitudes necessary to demonstrate their knowledge on all types of assessments, including norm-referenced tests.

We wrote this book because we believe that norm-referenced tests create inequities for specific groups of children and in many cases, misrepresent what they know and can do. Still, norm-referenced tests are not going away any time soon. This reality challenged us to find a way to co-opt the tests so they were less likely to act as barriers to educational opportunities. As we worked toward this goal, we honored the many ways children learn and construct meaning by keeping them at the center of our workshop approach. Developmental theory, critical inquiry, active and collaborative learning, and the interconnectedness of learning, teaching, and assessment guided our thinking. We hope that this book will be one of the tools educators use to make good on the promise of an American education.

APPENDIXES

Name: _____

Date: _____

Preassessment of Children's Attitudes and Experiences

What Do You Think About Tests?

1. I have taken multiple-choice tests before. **(Circle the letter of the *one* response that is most true for you.)**

    A. I'm not really sure what a multiple-choice test is.

    B. One or two times.

    C. Three or more times.

    D. Never.

2. The best description of my attitude toward multiple-choice tests is **(circle the letter of the *one* response that is most true for you):**

    A. Tests are fun! I like the challenge.

    B. Tests upset me! I get really worried.

    C. Tests are okay. They don't really bother me.

    D. Tests are boring. I don't like them.

    E. I don't care.

    F. I don't know. I've never taken a multiple-choice test before.

3. On a scale of 1 to 10, with 10 being REALLY GREAT! and 1 being REALLY BAD!, how well do you think you will do on the achievement tests you will take in a few weeks? **(Circle the number that describes how you think you will do.)**

1	2	3	4	5	6	7	8	9	10

REALLY
BAD!

REALLY
GREAT!

(over)

4. What I've heard about these achievement tests from grown-ups is **(circle one of the choices or write in your own answer):**

A. I haven't really heard anybody talk about them until today.

B. I heard they don't really matter. Somebody said we have to take them.

C. I heard they're pretty important.

D. I heard:

_____

_____

_____

_____

(Write what you heard about these tests if you didn't choose answer A, B, or C.)

5. Predict how you'll do on the achievement test! Which subject do you think you'll do BEST on? **(Circle only one!)**

A. Reading   B. Math   C. Science   D. Social Studies   E. Spelling   F. Language

G. I don't know which subject I'll do best on.

6. When you take a multiple-choice test, how do you figure out what answer to pick? **(Write how you decide which answer to choose on a multiple-choice test.)**

_____

_____

_____

_____

_____

_____

Practice Test 1

Directions: *For Questions 1–4, read the paragraph. Choose the word that goes with each numbered blank and best completes each sentence.*

Whales are the largest mammals on the earth, but they live in the sea. Many people visit aquariums to ___(1)___ whales because they think whales are fascinating. Some people are so interested in these ___(2)___ that they become scientists who study whales. At one time, whales were hunted almost to extinction, even though many scientists are sure they are quite ___(3)___. Scientists have discovered many interesting ___(4)___ about whales' intelligence. For example, they have found that some types of whales communicate through songs and that some whales hunt prey in packs. They have also discovered that whales have "aunties" who help when the babies are born.

1. A. swim   B. observe   C. trick   D. catch

2. A. fish   B. mammals   C. aquariums   D. stories

3. A. intelligent   B. stupid   C. funny   D. scared

4. A. lies   B. colors   C. names   D. facts

Directions: *Read the following story. Then do Questions 5–6. Choose the best response for each question.*

The violin is the smallest instrument in the violin "family." The viola, cello, and bass are the other instruments in the violin "family." The bass is the largest of the four instruments.

Violins have four strings that vibrate when a bow is drawn across them. The bow is made of a thin, round stick with long strands of horse hair attached. When the strings vibrate, the violin produces sound.

Violins are also called fiddles. Fiddle music is often played at dances and other social occasions.

5. Violins produce sound when:

A. they are called fiddles.

B. horse hair bows are used.

C. their strings vibrate.

D. they have four strings.

6. The author's purpose for writing this piece was to

A. instruct.

B. amuse.

C. persuade.

D. inform.

©1998 by Kathe Taylor and Sherry Walton from *Children at the Center*. Portsmouth, NH: Heinemann.

Directions: *For Question 7, read the meaning for the underlined Latin word and then choose the modern word that comes from the underlined Latin word. The Latin word and the modern word will be similar in meaning.*

7. Choose the word that comes from the Latin word <u>legalis</u>, which means "law."

A. legend   B. leg   C. legal   D. body

Directions: *For Question 8, choose the word that correctly completes both sentences.*

8. The boy will _____ his puppy.
The freight _____ carried apples and oranges in its boxcars.

A. wash   B. train   C. brush   D. walk

Directions: *For Question 9, choose the word that will go in both blanks to correctly complete the sentence.*

9. She couldn't _____ to watch the _____ jump through the ring of fire at the circus.

A. tiger   B. stand   C. bear   D. wait

Directions: *For Question 10, choose the word that means the opposite of the underlined word.*

10. The <u>furious</u> crow

A. black   B. angry   C. calm   D. loud

Directions: *For Question 11, choose the answer that best combines the two sentences into one sentence.*

11. Ashleigh walked to school. She kicked rocks as she walked.

A. Kicking Ashleigh rocked as she walked.

B. Ashleigh walked to school kicking rocks as she went.

C. The rocks Ashleigh kicked and walked to school.

D. Walking to school, Ashleigh kicking rocks.

Directions: *For Questions 12–22, choose the correct answers.*

12. 13 + 7 + 16 =

A. 46   B. 36   C. 55   D. 47

13. Kevin rode a bike every afternoon after school last week. Each ride took 45 minutes. Which of these number sentences could be used to find out how long Kevin rode the bike last week?

A. 9   B. 45 ÷ 5 =   C. 225   D. 45 x 5 =

14. 572
  − 223

  A. 349   B. 251   C. 379   D. 795

15. $159 \times 4 =$

  A. 436   B. 632   C. 636   D. 478

16. 44
  × 85

  A. 3140   B. 129   C. 329   D. 3740

17. $4\overline{)259}$

  A. 55 R2   B. 64 R3   C. 48   D. 64

18. $90 \div 30 =$

  A. 3   B. 30   C. 60   D. 4 R2

19. $2.3 + 0.8 =$

  A. 0.031   B. 0.31   C. 31   D. 3.1

20. $\frac{5}{7} - \frac{2}{7} =$

  A. $\frac{3}{7}$ B. $\frac{3}{5}$ C. $\frac{1}{7}$ D. $\frac{7}{5}$

21. Jason wanted to cook a spaghetti dinner for his family. He needed to buy two packages of spaghetti, which cost $ .98 each. He also needed to purchase two jars of sauce. The sauce cost $2.26 a jar. There are 5 people in Jason's family. What information is *not* needed to figure out how much the dinner would cost?

  A. The spaghetti cost $ .98 per package.

  B. Jason needed two packages of noodles and two packages of sauce.

  C. There are 5 people in Jason's family.

  D. Two jars of sauce cost $4.52.

22. Finish the pattern. Which number is missing?

  4, 20, _____, 500, 2500

  A. 100   B. 25   C. 250   D. 255

END OF TEST

Directions: *For Question 8, choose the word that correctly completes both sentences.*

8. The boy will _____ his puppy.

The freight _____ carried apples and oranges in its boxcars.

A. wash   B. train   C. brush   D. walk

CHOICES	TALLY OF RESPONSES
A. wash	
B. train	
C. brush	
D. walk	

Correct Response: B

Directions: *For Question 10, choose the word that means the opposite of the underlined word.*

10. The <u>furious</u> crow

    A. black   B. angry   C. calm   D. loud

CHOICES	TALLY OF RESPONSES
A. black	
B. angry	
C. calm	
D. loud	

Correct Response: C

Directions: *For Questions 12–22, choose the correct answers.*

12. $13 + 7 + 16 =$

A. 46   B. 36   C. 55   D. 47

CHOICES	TALLY OF RESPONSES
A. 46	
B. 36	
C. 55	
D. 47	

Correct Response: B

13. Kevin rode a bike every afternoon after school last week. Each ride took 45 minutes. Which of these number sentences could be used to find out how long Kevin rode the bike last week?

A. 9   B. 45 ÷ 5 =   C. 225   D. 45 × 5 =

CHOICES	TALLY OF RESPONSES
A. 9	
B. 45 ÷ 5 =	
C. 225	
D. 45 × 5 =	

Correct Response: D

©1998 by Kathe Taylor and Sherry Walton from *Children at the Center*. Portsmouth, NH: Heinemann.

Practice Test 2

Directions: *Choose the most accurate answer. Fill in the circle on your answer sheet that matches the letter of the answer you chose. Do NOT mark on this test.*

23. Which of the following statements is accurate about the perimeters of these rectangles?

4 cm

3 cm   X

5 cm

2 cm   Y

A. The perimeters are the same.

B. The perimeter of rectangle X is greater.

C. The perimeter of rectangle Y is greater.

D. There is no way to figure out the perimeters.

24. In this box, the numbers added across, down, and diagonally equal 15. What two numbers are missing?

	1	8
7	5	3
	9	4

A. 6 and 5

B. 7 and 3

C. 6 and 2

D. 6 and 4

25. 5137 − 2253 = ☐

A. 2885

B. 2874

C. 2783

D. 2884

Directions: *The bar graph below shows the favorite snack for Ms. Walton's fourth-grade students. Use the graph to choose the most accurate response to Questions 26 and 27.*

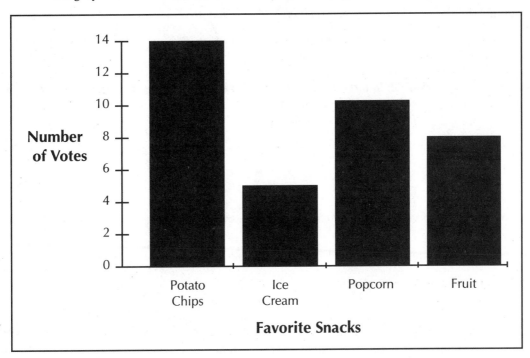

26. How many students voted for popcorn?

A. 5   B. 8   C. 10   D. 12

27. Which snack do the fourth-graders like least of all?

A. potato chips   B. ice cream   C. popcorn   D. none of these

28. Which of these would you measure in meters?

A. the length of your finger

B. the length of the hall in your school

C. the width of a book

D. I don't use meters.

29. Perimeter equals the sum of a figure's sides. What is the perimeter of the square below?

A. 16 inches

B. 8 inches

C. 4 inches

D. 32 inches

4 inches

4 inches

30. $8\overline{)145}$

A. 17 R2   B. 17 R4   C. 18 R5   D. none of the above

Directions: *For Question 31, choose the best answer to complete the sentence.*

31. Last night, Raitha _____ her mother's rollerblades.

    A. break   B. broke   C. will break   D. has broken

Directions: *For Question 32, find the word with the correct spelling that best completes the sentence.*

32. Daniel _____ the whole doughnut.

    A. ait   B. eight   C. ate   D. ayt

Directions: *For Question 33, choose the most accurate answer.*

33. Where would you most likely find a large map of Spain?

    A. encyclopedia   B. almanac   C. atlas   D. dictionary

Directions: *The line in the paragraph below means a sentence is missing. Choose the sentence that is missing from the paragraph to answer Question 34.*

34. Taylor loves to garden with her grandfather. They put on their gloves and take their shovels to the back yard. As her grandfather watches, Taylor begins digging a hole with her shovel. _____. She plants the seeds in the earth, and covers the seeds with the pile of loose dirt.

    A. Taylor her shovel.

    B. Taylor shovels the dirt into a pile.

    C. Taylor puts on her gloves.

    D. Taylor pats the earth over the seeds.

Directions: *Read the following story to answer Question 35.*

Amelia Earhart was born in Atchison, Kansas, in 1897. Her family gave her the nickname "Millie." Amelia loved books, animals, and the outdoors. She grew up to be the first woman pilot to fly across the Atlantic Ocean. She flew many long distances at a time when air travel was still new. Her plane disappeared when she tried to fly around the world.

35. Which statement below is an opinion?

    A. Amelia grew up in Atchison, Kansas.

    B. Amelia was the first woman to fly across the Atlantic Ocean.

    C. Amelia tried to fly around the world.

    D. Amelia was one of the best pilots of all time.

END OF TEST

Answers to Practice Test Questions

Practice Test 1

1. B		**12.** B	
2. B		**13.** D	
3. A		**14.** A	
4. D		**15.** C	
5. C		**16.** D	
6. D		**17.** B	
7. C		**18.** A	
8. B		**19.** D	
9. C		**20.** A	
10. C		**21.** C	
11. B		**22.** A	

Practice Test 2

23. A		**30.** D	
24. C		**31.** B	
25. D		**32.** C	
26. C		**33.** C	
27. B		**34.** B	
28. B		**35.** D	
29. A			

Name: _____

Date: _____

Postassessment of Children's Attitudes and Experiences

So, What Did You Think?

We're interested in knowing if practicing test strategies helped you with the test you just finished taking. Please take a few minutes to answer these questions and tell us about your experiences.

1. Do you think practicing some of the different kinds of problem-solving strategies ahead of time helped you with the test? **(Circle *one* response.)**

   A. Yes! It helped a lot.

   B. Yes! It helped some.

   C. No! It didn't help.

2. Do you think practicing ahead of time helped you feel calmer and less worried about taking the test? **(Circle *one* response.)**

   A. Yes! I think practicing helped me feel less worried when I took the test.

   B. No! I don't think practicing helped me feel any less worried.

   C. No! I think practicing made me feel *more* worried.

   D. No! I wasn't worried to begin with.

3. On a scale of 1 to 10, with 10 being REALLY GREAT! and 1 being REALLY BAD!, how well do you think you did on the tests overall? **(Circle the number that describes how you think you did.)**

1	2	3	4	5	6	7	8	9	10
REALLY BAD!									REALLY GREAT!

4. Which test do you think you did the best on? _____

(over)

5. Please circle *every* problem-solving strategy you used to help you with the tests.

A. I used the "begin with what you know" strategy. I went through the test and tried to answer every question I knew first.

B. On test items I wasn't sure of, I used the "process of elimination" strategy and eliminated wrong answers first.

C. When I didn't know what a word meant, I tried to look for other clues that would help me with the question.

D. I made sure that the number on the test question was the same as the number on the bubble answer sheet.

E. For spelling words, I tried to write or imagine the way I thought the word was spelled *before* I looked at the list of answers.

F. I read each question carefully and looked for key words. I tried to make sure that I understood what each question was asking me to do.

G. I didn't worry when I heard other people turning pages of the test because I knew that they were probably using the "begin with what you know" strategy.

H. On the reading passages and for the story problems in math, I read the question *before* I read the passages or the story problem.

6. Please list any other problem-solving strategies you used to help yourself.

_____

_____

7. Circle the workshop activities you think *helped you the most* with the tests you just finished taking. **(You can circle more than one.)**

A. Taking the practice tests, because it helped me know what to expect.

B. Talking about the reasons kids might choose different answers to the questions.

C. Practicing different problem-solving strategies.

D. Talking about the way we *felt* when we took the tests.

E. Just getting used to filling out the bubble answer sheets.

8. Write down one or two examples of ways you could use some of the problem-solving strategies we discussed to try to figure out something you don't know when you're *not* taking a test.

_____

_____

©1998 by Kathe Taylor and Sherry Walton from *Children at the Center*. Portsmouth, NH: Heinemann.

Bibliography

Bond, Linda A., Edward D. Roeber, and David Braskamp. 1996. *Trends in State Student Assessment Programs.* Washington, D.C.: Council of Chief State School Officers.

Cannell, John J. 1988. "Nationally Normed Elementary Achievement Testing in America's Public Schools: How All 50 States Are Above the National Average." *Educational Measurement: Issues and Practice* (Summer): 5–9.

"Guidelines for Appropriate Curriculum Content and Assessment in Programs Serving Children Ages 3 Through 8." 1991. *Young Children* (March): 21–38.

Herman, Joan L., Jamal Abedi, and Shari Golan. 1994. "Assessing the Effects of Standardized Testing on Schools." *Educational and Psychological Measurement* 52: 471–482.

McAuliffe, Sheila. 1993. "A Study of the Differences Between Instructional Practice and Test Preparation." *Journal of Reading* 36: 524–530.

Mehrens, William A., and John Kaminski. 1989. "Methods of Improving Standardized Test Scores: Fruitful, Fruitless, or Fraudulent?" *Educational Measurement: Issues and Practice* (Spring): 114–122.

"National Association for the Education of Young Children Position Statement on Standardized Testing of Young Children 3 Through 8 Years of Age." 1988. *Young Children* (March): 42–47.

National Commission on Testing and Public Policy. 1990. *From Gatekeeper to Gateway: Transforming Testing in America.* Chestnut Hill, MA: National Commission on Testing and Public Policy.

National Public Radio. 1998. "State of Education II." *All Things Considered.* January 26.

Nolen, Susan B., Thomas M. Haladyna, and Nancy S. Haas. 1992. "Uses and Abuses of Achievement Test Scores." *Educational Measurement: Issues and Practice* (Summer): 9–16.

Paris, Scott G., et al. 1991. "A Developmental Perspective on Standardized Achievement Testing." *Educational Researcher* (June/July): 12–20.

Popham, W. James. 1995. *Classroom Assessment*. Needham Heights, MA: Allyn and Bacon.

Resnick, Lauren B., and Daniel P. Resnick. 1989. "Tests as Standards of Achievement in School." *Proceedings of the 1989 ETS Invitational Conference: The Uses of Standardized Tests in American Education*. Princeton, NJ: Educational Testing Service.

Rothman, Robert. 1995. *Measuring Up*. San Francisco: Jossey-Bass.

Scruggs, Thomas E., Karl R. White, and Karla Bennion. 1986. "Teaching Test-Taking Skills to Elementary-Grade Students: A Meta-Analysis." *The Elementary School Journal* 87: 69–82.

Smith, Mary L. 1991. "Meanings of Test Preparation." *American Educational Research Journal* 28: 521–542.

Stewart, Edward C., and Milton J. Bennett. 1991. *American Cultural Patterns*. Yarmouth, ME: Intercultural Press.

Thomas, Wayne P., and Virginia Collier. 1997. "School Effectiveness for Language Minority Students." National Clearinghouse for Bilingual Education Resource Collection Series, No. 9, December. Washington, D.C.: The George Washington University Center for the Study of Language and Education.

Urdan, Timothy C., and Scott G. Paris. 1994. "Teachers' Perceptions of Standardized Achievement Tests." *Educational Policy* 8: 137–156.